P9-ARH-770

Betty White's

DANCING MADE EASY

By the same author

BETTY WHITE'S
TEEN-AGE DANCE BOOK

Betty White's

DANCING MADE EASY

illustrated by
ROBERT BURNS

DAVID McKAY COMPANY, INC.

New York

Dedicated to
Anita Peters Wright

Acknowledgments

THE author acknowledges her appreciation to the members of the staff of the Dominican Republic Consulate for their assistance in providing bibliography for the merengue. Furthermore, the author is indebted to Mr. Guillermo Nadal for his patience and enthusiasm—both as a performer and adviser—in the recording of the dance.

Thanks are also due Dr. Enrique de Marchena, outstanding Dominican musicologist, for his assistance in reading the manuscript for the merengue.

And finally, an acknowledgment would be incomplete without some mention of Dr. Manuel Sanchez, well-known Dominican composer, for his interest in analyzing and checking the musical rhythms.

B. W.

Contents

CONTENTS

CONTENTS

CONTENTS

CONTENTS

Betty White's

DANCING MADE EASY

1. Introduction

DO you know how to dance? If you don't, let's do something about it. There are numerous occasions when you will wish you knew how to dance—parties to which you will be invited where everyone is dancing, or you may find yourself in the position of entertaining business acquaintances in restaurants where there is dancing. In any event, if you can dance, your opportunities for meeting and mixing with other people will be greatly enhanced.

In addition, you will find dancing mentally and physically relaxing. It will help you to develop a sense of rhythm. And with the knowledge that you can dance well will come more poise and confidence.

A good, all-around dancer is always popular and sought after. And last but not least, dancing is *fun!*

HOW TO USE THIS BOOK

Every chapter has been so arranged that you can progress from the easy steps to the more difficult figures. If you already know a particular dance, go on to the next one. Be sure, however, that you have mastered one dance before proceeding to another. And remember to practice until you can do a dance with perfect ease.

2. Preparation

MOVING IN THE LINE OF DIRECTION

BEFORE practicing a specific dance it might be well for you to become familiar with a few general rules for social dancing.

In progressing around the floor, couples move counterclockwise.

And although the customary line of direction is counterclockwise, a certain amount of freedom is permitted in moving about the floor. One may move either forward, backward, or sideward.

Good posture should be maintained by both the woman and man—the torso easy but erect, the weight of the body over the balls of the feet—while standing or practicing. A simple, natural style of dancing should be observed.

At all times a man should keep aware of his relationship to other couples on the floor, since he assumes the initiative of leading and steering. He, in other words, assumes entire responsibility for his partner. He should, therefore, know how to dance and, what is equally important, what is good social custom while at a dance.

LEADING AND FOLLOWING

A man should indicate his steps and leads sufficiently in advance so that a woman can follow with confidence. A woman, in turn, should keep relaxed so she can respond immediately to a lead.

The technique for leading and following in the line of direction will be described in detail under the section "Positions in Dancing." These positions are used in the so-called progressive dances, for example, the waltz. In addition, however, to using forward or backward steps, most of these dances include side steps. It will be necessary, therefore, at this point to describe the side leads.

To move the woman to the *left* (her right), the man's right palm exerts a gentle but firm pressure against the left side of the woman's torso.

To move the woman to the *right* (her left), the man pulls the woman's torso gently to the right with the upper right arm and hand.

The signal for changing from a forward to a side direction must be given in advance so that the man and woman "push off" simultaneously. To indicate the lead for the side steps, the right hand is slipped from under the shoulder blade to the left side of the woman's torso. And the weight of the body should be kept well over the balls of the feet so that any change in direction can be made easily.

And, finally, to move backward (as the woman moves forward), the man pulls the woman toward him with the right hand, which is under her left shoulder blade.

Eventually leads will become so automatic that you will not have to think of them. But until they do, remember the right hand acts more or less as a rudder in steering the woman in or out of any figure. Therefore, a gentle but firm pressure should be maintained by the right hand—at all times. Most important!

SOME DANCE DEFINITIONS

It will also be necessary for you to become familiar with a few dance terms.

A step involves a complete transference of the weight of the body from one foot to the other.

A figure consists of a fixed number of steps done in succession.

A lead is a pressure of the hand, shoulder, or entire body to indicate the beginning or end of a figure. A lead may also indicate a change of direction.

Rhythm—"quick" or "slow" is purely relative and refers to beats in music and the steps taken to those beats.

"Quick" has a time duration of one beat and occupies approximately the length of time it takes to say the single word "quick."

"Slow" has a time duration of two beats and approximates the length of time required to say the two words "quick, quick" in succession.

Follow-through is the principle of the feet remaining parallel to each other in passing from one step to another (inside edge of soles almost touching) and the drawing up of the active foot against the supporting foot on completing a step or beginning a new one. Dotted lines on the floor diagram will indicate this movement. It is the follow-through principle that makes for a narrow base. Most important.

Floor diagram is a pattern of imaginary lines describing the tracks made on the floor by the feet in stepping or following through.

Style is the manner in which a dance is done.

MUSIC

Since the radio and phonograph have already made you familiar with foxtrot vocals known nationally as top tunes, you will find it easier to start practicing to foxtrot music.

Get yourself a good, standard dance album that has a solid

beat and which maintains a comfortable walking pace to dance to —not too slow and not too fast. Listen carefully for the four beats in each measure in the foxtrot. Usually the beats are accented by drums, "brushes," or a bass fiddle. Tapping with the feet or clapping hands will help you keep time. If you find it easier to move around the room while listening—do! But be sure to step on each beat.

The same procedure will hold for the rumba, mambo, tango, charleston, one-step, merengue, lindy, samba, polka, and calypso, since all of those dances are done in 4/4 time. And, of course, you know that there are three beats to a measure in a waltz.

STANDARD DANCE BANDS FOR PRACTICE

Foxtrot or Lindy

Glenn Miller
Tommy Dorsey
Les Brown
Harry James
Benny Goodman
Guy Lombardo
Ray Anthony
Les Elgart

Waltz

Al Goodman
Lawrence Welk
Guy Lombardo

Rumba

Noro Morales
Xavier Cugat
Emil Coleman

Mambo and Cha Cha Cha

Tito Puente
Perez Prado
Machito
Tito Rodriques

Merengue

Angel Viloria
Al Castellanos
Ricardo Rico

Tango

Pancho
Marek Weber
Xavier Cugat

Samba

Luis Oliveira
Xavier Cugat

Paso Doble

Los Chavales de España
Leal Pescador

Charleston

Eddie Condon
Pee Wee Hunt

Polka

Frankie Yankovic
"Whoopee" John Wilfahrt
Lawrence Welk

Marches

Sousa—American
Legion Band
Edwin Franko Goldman

Calypso

Harry Belafonte
The Mighty Zebra
The Duke of Iron

Consult your local dealer for recent releases.

PRACTICE

Before you start practicing a dance, glance over the descriptive material and floor diagram.

Study the descriptive section carefully. Try to get a mental picture of what the step is like. If you find it easier, walk through the description while you read it—or make yourself a diagram on the floor. Although you may not find it necessary to make floor diagrams, use any method that enables you to practice with confidence.

Take one dance at a time.

Practice one figure at a time.

Start practice from a base, as shown in the diagram:

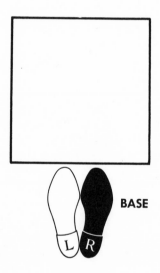

Feet parallel: inside edge of soles touching, weight of body over the balls of feet, toes pointing straight ahead. Feet remain parallel at all times progressing forward, backward, sideward, and turning.

Call out a rhythm while you practice (for example: the fox-trot—slow, slow, quick, quick). Practice a step until you get a feeling for what the rhythm is like.

If it is easier for you to practice to music, do so at once.

As soon as you have learned a step, start practicing with a partner immediately. But do not practice with a partner until you know your own step.

When you really get going, try making up your own combinations. Watch what the other dancers are doing and change partners occasionally.

And don't forget. As soon as you have learned one step, go to a dance. Remember, "Practice makes perfect!"

3. Positions in Dancing

THERE are *four* positions in dancing: the closed position, the open or promenade position, the side or step-out position, the skater's position or a variation of the skater's position. Each of the four positions will be described in detail and illustrated.

It is most important for you to study these positions *carefully* so that you will be thoroughly familiar with them when they are used in the instructions for the individual dances. Be sure to give full attention, in studying each position, to the paragraphs headed "Leading the Woman" and "Following the Man" (and also reread the earlier section on "Leading and Following" under "Preparation") so that you will master the principles of leading and following right from the start.

After taking up the four basic dance positions we will illustrate and describe the positions of the hands for the various dances. And then we will proceed to the dances themselves.

Remember to turn back to these preliminary pages on positions for reference whenever you need to review them.

parst,

CLOSED POSITION

The Man

Stand in front of your partner, feet together, pointing straight in the line of direction (counterclockwise), weight of the body over the ball of the right foot only. Left foot parallel with right foot. Inside edge of soles touching.

The right hand is held below the woman's left shoulder blade, palm facing in. The left hand clasps the woman's right hand with the arm extended in a curve, slightly below shoulder level.

Although shoulders remain parallel, the head is turned slightly to your left. You do have to see where you are going, you know. Now, you are ready to lead.

Leading the Woman

Moving forward in the closed position calls for a chest lead. That is, the upper torso pushes forward to back the woman into the line of direction.

CLOSED POSITION

The Woman

Stand in front of your partner, feet together, toes just clearing tips of man's shoes, weight of the body over the ball of the left foot only. Right foot parallel with left foot. Inside edge of soles touching.

The left hand rests gently but firmly on the man's right shoulder. The right hand rests vertically in the man's left palm—palm facing in—the right arm extending in a curve slightly below shoulder level.

Although the shoulders remain parallel, the head is turned slightly to your left so that the man can look straight ahead in the line of direction. Now, you are ready to follow.

Following the Man

As soon as you have sensed the pressure of the man's lead, to back you into the line of direction, reach back with the big toe in a straight line from the hip. Transfer the weight gradually.

THE PROMENADE

The Man

With the left side facing the line of direction (counterclockwise) stand sideward with the woman on your right side—feet together, weight of the body over the ball of the right foot only. Left foot parallel with right foot. Inside edge of soles touching.

The right hand is held at the left side of the woman's torso, palm facing in. The left hand clasps the woman's right hand with the arm extended in a curve, slightly below shoulder level.

The head and shoulders are turned slightly to your left so that you are looking straight ahead in the line of direction. Both you and the woman are now in a partially open position.

Leading the Woman

Moving forward in the promenade position calls for a side lead. The right hand pushes gently against the left side of the woman's torso to indicate the forward movement. And since both you and the woman are facing the line of direction, the initial lead and step will be taken almost simultaneously.

THE PROMENADE

The Woman

With the right side facing the line of direction (counterclockwise) stand sideward on the man's right side—feet together, toes just clearing tips of man's shoes, weight of the body over the ball of the left foot only. Right foot parallel with left foot. Inside edge of soles touching.

The left hand rests gently but firmly on the man's right shoulder. The right hand rests vertically in the man's left palm—palm facing in—the right arm extending in a curve slightly below shoulder level.

The head and shoulders are turned slightly to your right so

that you are looking straight ahead in the line of direction. Both you and the man are now in partially open position.

Following the Man

You will find it quite easy to follow through on the first step as soon as the side lead is given by the man—a gentle forward push against the left side of the torso in the line of direction.

SIDE OR STEP-OUT POSITION

The Man

Stand with your partner on your right side, facing in the line of direction. (The woman is standing with her back in the line of direction so the position is right side to right side.) Feet together, weight of the body over the ball of the right foot only. Left foot parallel with right foot. Inside edge of soles touching.

The right hand is held at the left side of the woman's torso,

palm facing in. The left hand clasps the woman's right hand with the arm extended in a curve, slightly below shoulder level.

Look straight ahead in the line of direction.

Leading the Woman

Moving forward in the line of direction in the side or step-out position (so called because the man steps out to the side to begin a step) calls for an initial lead from both the chest and upper right arm. A slight pressure of the left hand against the woman's right hand will help to maintain the lead. NOTE: The side or step-out position may be done left side to left side by merely moving the woman from the right to the left side.

SIDE OR STEP-OUT POSITION

The Woman

With your back in the line of direction stand at the right side of the man. (The man is facing in the line of direction so the position is right side to right side.) Feet together, weight of the body over the ball of the left foot only. Right foot parallel with left foot. Inside edge of soles touching.

The left hand rests gently but firmly on the man's right shoulder. The right hand rests vertically in the man's left palm—palm facing in—the right arm extending in a curve slightly below shoulder level.

Look straight ahead.

Following the Man

You will feel an initial lead from both the chest and the upper right arm as the man backs you into the line of direction. A slight pressure of the man's left hand against your right hand will enable you to continue following.

SKATER'S POSITION

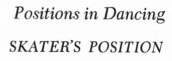

Man and Woman

Facing in the line of direction, stand side by side (man's right side against woman's left side), weight over the balls of the feet; cross arms, joining right hand with right hand, left hand with left hand.

Leading the Woman

With the hands clasped, gently pull the woman forward in the line of direction.

VARIATION OF THE SKATER'S POSITION

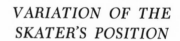

Man and Woman

Facing in the line of direction, with the woman's left shoulder against the man's right shoulder, stand with the weight over the balls of the feet. Arms bent at the elbows, hands held at shoulder level (the woman's hands held vertically—palms facing out), join left hand with left hand, right hand with right hand, palms facing in.

Leading the Woman

Push the woman into the line of direction from the chest.

POSITIONS OF THE HANDS

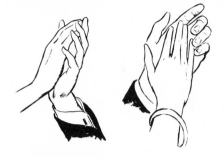

1. *The Vertical Hand Position*

The man holds the woman's right hand in his left hand vertically, the palms facing in. (The vertical hand position is used in the following dances: foxtrot, waltz, one-step, tango, samba, and Viennese waltz.)

2. *Rumba and Mambo Hand Position*

The man holds the woman's right hand in his left, the thumb pressing vertically against the inside of her palm, with the second and third fingers clasping the back of her hand. (To pull the woman in after a "break," the fourth and fifth fingers are pressed down against her wrist.)

3. *Lindy Hand Position*

With the fingers crossed, facing in (the woman's fingers pointing down), the man holds the woman's right hand in his left, the thumb pressing just below the woman's knuckles.

4. Foxtrot

ALTHOUGH there are several varieties of foxtrots, the medium-slow is still the most popular. And probably the easiest and most relaxing to do.

The music calls for smooth, gliding movements, so try to cultivate long, continuous steps. Bands all over the country provide an opportunity for "dancing out," and for practice, ample opportunity will be found through the use of records. There are numerous recordings of all the old favorites as well as recent releases. Be sure, however, to keep a smooth, easy style while dancing to America's favorite—the medium-slow foxtrot.

THE BASIC RHYTHM

The basic rhythm of the medium-slow foxtrot is 4/4 time with the first and third beats accented ♩ ♩ ♩ ♩ . We have an even more interesting rhythm, however, in the medium-slow foxtrot, known as slow, slow, quick, quick.

Two half notes 𝅗𝅥 𝅗𝅥 followed by two quarter notes ♩ ♩ give us 𝅗𝅥 𝅗𝅥 ♩ ♩ —our slow, slow, quick, quick rhythm. In counting the beats, however, we find an overlapping of the rhythm within a 4/4 measure. Here is what it looks like:

PRACTICING THE FOXTROT

Two slow steps are taken followed by two quick steps in dancing to the medium-slow foxtrot. By merely changing one's direction or position any number of fascinating combinations can be devised.

We are starting off with the more basic figures, the closed position, the promenade, the dip, and the turn-under (promenade). Later, we will progress to the zigzag and half turns. Some mention will be made regarding the running step. Each of these figures is described.

In learning the figures, start off with the closed position and progress to the promenade. The dip may follow, and for something a little tricky, you will find it easy to progress to the turn-under.

After you have practiced the individual figures you can begin to combine them. Progressing from the closed position to the dip, for example, will be simple since you are already in closed position. And the transition from the promenade to the turn-under can be made just as easily.

The transitions (moving from one figure into another) can be done quite readily on the quick, quick steps. The last quick of the figure you are doing is used for changing to a new figure.

And be sure, after you get going, to try some combinations of your own.

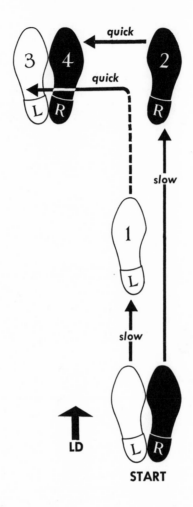

4. Close right foot against left foot, transferring weight, quick (1 count).

3. Step to left side with left foot, quick (1 count).

2. Step forward on right foot, slow (2 counts). (Draw left foot up to right—follow dotted line.)

1. Step forward on left foot, slow (2 counts).

Man

MEDIUM-SLOW FOXTROT—CLOSED POSITION

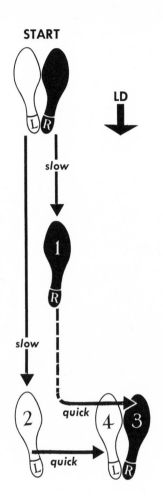

Woman

1. Step backward on right foot, slow (2 counts).

2. Step backward on left foot, slow (2 counts). (Draw right foot back to left—follow dotted line.)

3. Step to right side with right foot, quick (1 count).

4. Close left foot against right foot, transferring weight, quick (1 count).

MEDIUM-SLOW FOXTROT—CLOSED POSITION

Man

1. Step forward on left foot.

2. Step forward on right foot.

3. Step to left side with left foot.

4. Close right foot against left foot, transferring weight.

(Woman follows man.)

MEDIUM-SLOW FOXTROT—CLOSED POSITION

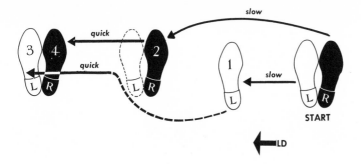

Man

1. Step sideways on left foot, slow (2 counts).

2. Step across in front of the left foot with right foot, slow (2 counts). (Draw left foot up to right—follow dotted line.)

3. Step sideways on left foot, quick (1 count).

4. Close right foot against left foot, transferring weight, quick (1 count).

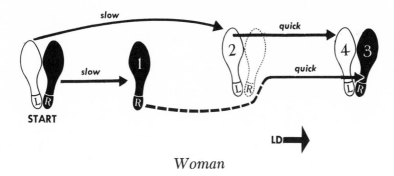

Woman

1. Step sideways on right foot, slow (2 counts).

2. Step across in front of the right foot with left foot, slow (2 counts). (Draw right foot up to left foot—follow dotted line.)

3. Step sideways on right foot, quick (1 count).

4. Close left foot against right foot, transferring weight, quick (1 count).

PROMENADE
MEDIUM-SLOW FOXTROT

Man

1. Step sideways on the left foot.

2. Step across with right foot.

3. Step sideways on left foot.

4. Close right foot against left foot, transferring weight.

(Woman follows man.)

PROMENADE
MEDIUM-SLOW FOXTROT

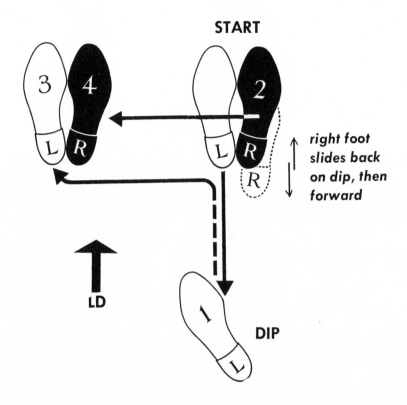

Man

1. Step back on the left foot, bending at the knee, right leg extended, slow (2 counts).

2. Step forward on the right foot, slow (2 counts). (Draw left foot up to right—follow dotted line.)

3. Step to left side with left foot, quick (1 count).

4. Close right foot against left foot, transferring weight, quick (1 count).

DIP
MEDIUM-SLOW FOXTROT

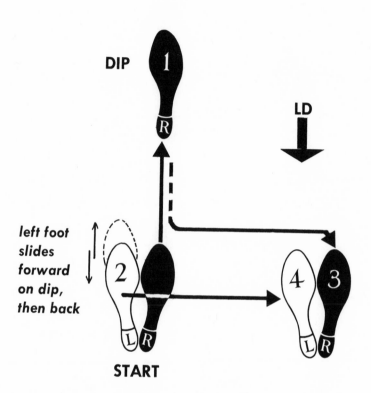

Woman

1. Step forward on the right foot, bending at the knee, left leg extended, slow (2 counts).

2. Step back on the left foot, slow (2 counts). (Draw right foot back to left—follow dotted line.)

3. Step to the right side with right foot, quick (1 count).

4. Close left foot against right foot, transferring weight, quick (1 count).

DIP
MEDIUM-SLOW FOXTROT

Man

1. Step back on the left foot.

2. Step forward on the right foot.

3. Step to left side with left foot.

4. Close right foot against left foot, transferring weight.

NOTE: The figure we have just described can be used as a right turn by the man pivoting to the right as he steps forward on his right foot, the woman pivoting to the right as she steps back on her left foot.

DIP
MEDIUM-SLOW FOXTROT

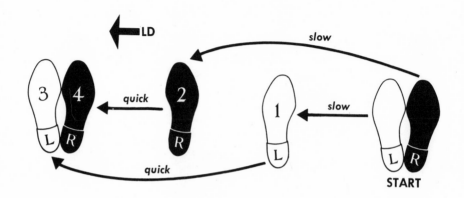

Man

1. Step sideways on left foot, slow (2 counts).

2. Step across in front of the left foot with right foot, slow (2 counts), with hands clasped, raise the woman's right arm to prepare for the right turn.

3. Step sideways on left foot, quick (1 count), turning the woman under her right arm and releasing your right hand.

4. Close right foot against left foot, transferring weight, quick (1 count), while bringing the right hand back to the left side of the woman's torso as she completes the turn; lower arms to shoulder level.

THE TURN-UNDER
(PROMENADE)
MEDIUM-SLOW FOXTROT

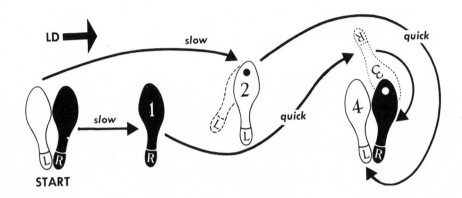

Woman

1. Step sideways on right foot, slow (2 counts).

2. Step across in front of the right foot with left foot, pivoting slightly to the right, slow (2 counts), raising the right arm to prepare for the right turn.

3. Step sideways, pivoting (turning) on ball of right foot (left foot follows through), making a complete right turn, quick (1 count), right fingers turning in man's left hand, while releasing left hand from man's right shoulder (keeping hands vertical while turning).

4. Close left foot against right foot, transferring weight, quick (1 count), drop left hand to man's right shoulder; lower arms to shoulder level.

THE TURN-UNDER
(PROMENADE)
MEDIUM-SLOW FOXTROT

Man

1. Step sideways on the left foot.

2. Step across with right foot.

3. Step sideways on left foot, turn woman under.

4. Close right foot against left foot, transferring weight.

THE TURN-UNDER
(PROMENADE)
MEDIUM-SLOW FOXTROT

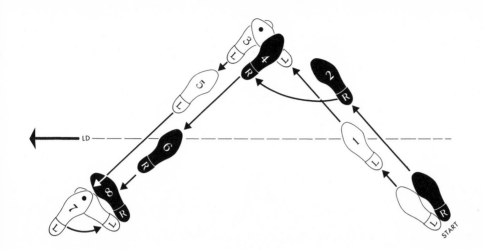

Man

Standing sideways, diagonally left in the line of direction, feet together, the weight over the ball of the right foot.

Forward diagonal:

1. Step forward on left foot, slow (2 counts).

2. Step forward on right foot, slow (2 counts).

3. Step forward on left foot, pivoting slightly to the right, quick (1 count).

4. Close right foot against left foot, transferring weight, quick (1 count).

Backward diagonal:

5. Step back on left foot, slow (2 counts).

6. Step back on right foot, slow (2 counts).

7. Step back on left foot, pivoting slightly to the left, quick (1 count).

8. Close right foot against left foot, transferring weight, quick (1 count).

ZIGZAG
MEDIUM-SLOW FOXTROT

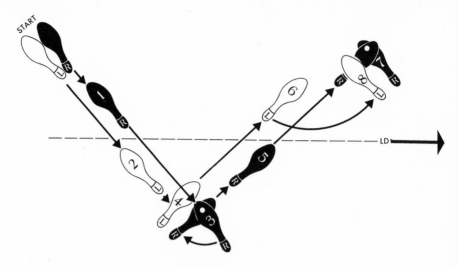

Woman

Standing sideways, diagonally left in the line of direction, feet together, weight over the ball of the left foot.

Backward diagonal:

1. Step back on right foot, slow (2 counts).

2. Step back on left foot, slow (2 counts).

3. Step back on right foot, pivoting slightly to the right, quick (1 count).

4. Close left foot against right foot, transferring weight, quick (1 count).

Forward diagonal:

5. Step forward on right foot, slow (2 counts).

6. Step forward on left foot, slow (2 counts).

7. Step forward on right foot, pivoting slightly to the left, quick (1 count).

8. Close left foot against right foot, transferring weight, quick (1 count).

ZIGZAG
MEDIUM-SLOW FOXTROT

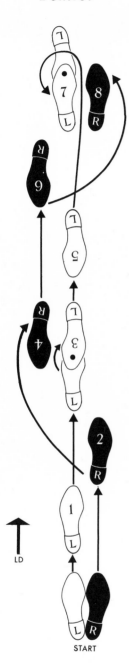

Man

Facing in the line of direction, feet together, the weight over the ball of the right foot.

Forward half turn:

1. Step forward on left foot, slow (2 counts).

2. Step forward on right foot, slow (2 counts).

3. Tightening your hold, step forward on left foot, pivoting a half turn to the right, quick (1 count).

4. Close right foot against left foot, transferring weight, quick (1 count).

Backward half turn:

5. Step back on left foot, slow (2 counts).

6. Step back on right foot, slow (2 counts).

7. Tightening your hold, step back on left foot, pivoting a half turn to the left, quick (1 count).

8. Close right foot against left foot, transferring weight, quick (1 count).

Turn the book in your hand to correspond with the direction in which you are moving.

HALF TURNS
MEDIUM-SLOW
FOXTROT

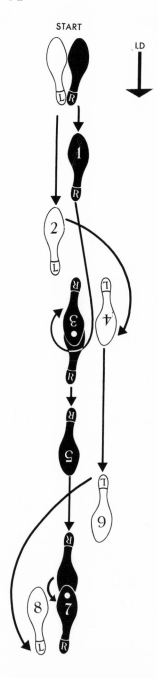

START

LD

Turn the book in your hand to correspond with the direction in which you are moving.

Woman

Backing in the line of direction, feet together, the weight over the ball of the left foot.

Backward half turn:

1. Step back on right foot, slow (2 counts).

2. Step back on left foot, slow (2 counts).

3. Arching the back slightly, step back on right foot, pivoting a half turn to the right, quick (1 count).

4. Close left foot against right foot, transferring weight, quick (1 count).

Forward half turn:

5. Step forward on right foot, slow (2 counts).

6. Step forward on left foot, slow (2 counts).

7. Arching the back slightly, step forward on right foot, pivoting a half turn to the left, quick (1 count).

8. Close left foot against right foot, transferring weight, quick (1 count).

HALF TURNS
MEDIUM-SLOW
FOXTROT

THE RUNNING STEP

Up to this point the figures described in the quick, quick rhythm of the medium-slow foxtrot have consisted of side steps, with which you are now familiar. And however much pleasure you may have derived from dancing the preceding figures, you will find the running step in the medium-slow foxtrot even more intriguing.

The figure consists of two walking steps (slow, slow) followed by two running steps (quick, quick) in the line of direction. The step may be done in any of the basic dance positions, although it is more characteristic when done in closed position. The running steps are taken lightly on the balls of the feet from a *strong* push-off from the second slow. It will be necessary, therefore, for the man to tighten his hold on the push-off.

In practicing the running step *both* the man and the woman should hold the torso erect while maintaining a smooth, gliding movement.

THE FOXTROT SQUARE

Here is a foxtrot figure that differs from the slow, slow, quick, quick. It is known as the square and is based on a slow, quick, quick rhythm.

Here it is:

Starting and returning to the same place, a square includes four directions—forward, sideward, backward, and sideward. See pages 37–38. The basic step of the square consists of a slow step forward followed by two quick steps to the side, and a slow step back followed by two quick steps to the side. Two measures of music are required in 4/4 ♩ ♩ ♩ ♩ time to complete the figure (eight beats).

Left Turn

We have just described the square in the foxtrot. Later we will proceed to use the square in a left turn. It will be necessary, however, for you to master the square before proceeding to the turn.

In addition to using the turn as an interesting dance figure, it has a practical value. It can be used to mark time when one is blocked off on a crowded floor and in rounding corners.

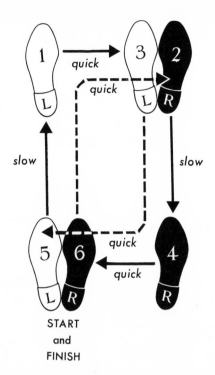

START
and
FINISH

6. Close right foot against left foot, transferring weight, quick (1 count).

5. Follow through with the left foot and step to left side, quick (1 count).

4. Step back on right foot, slow (2 counts).

3. Close left foot against right foot, transferring weight, quick (1 count).

2. Follow through with the right foot and step to the right side, quick (1 count).

1. Step forward on left foot, slow (2 counts).

(Follow dotted line for the follow-through.)

Man

THE SQUARE
FOXTROT—CLOSED POSITION

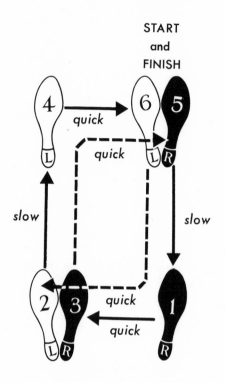

Woman

(Follow dotted line for the follow-through.)

1. Step backward on right foot, slow (2 counts).

2. Follow through with the left foot and step to the left side, quick (1 count).

3. Close right foot against left foot, transferring weight, quick (1 count).

4. Step forward on left foot, slow (2 counts).

5. Follow through with the right foot and step to right side, quick (1 count).

6. Close left foot against right foot, transferring weight, quick (1 count).

THE SQUARE
FOXTROT—CLOSED POSITION

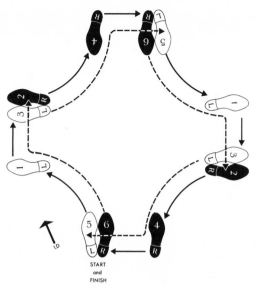

Turn the book in your hand to correspond with the direction in which you are turning.

(You have now done a half turn. To complete the turn repeat 1 through 6.)

6. Close right foot against left foot, transferring weight, quick (1 count).
5. Follow through with the left foot and step to left side, quick (1 count).
4. Continuing to turn left, pulling the woman toward you, step backward on right foot (heel leading), slow (2 counts).
3. Close left foot against right foot, transferring weight, quick (1 count).
2. Follow through with the right foot and step to right side, quick (1 count).
1. Chest lead, holding woman firmly with right hand while turning left, step forward on left foot, slow (2 counts).

(Follow dotted line for the follow-through.)

Man

LEFT TURN
FOXTROT—CLOSED POSITION

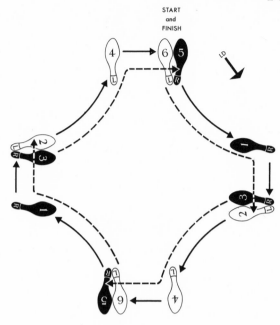

Turn the book in your hand to correspond with the direction in which you are turning.

Woman

(Follow dotted line for the follow-through.)

1. Step backward on right foot (heel leading), chest turning left, slow (2 counts).
2. Follow through with the left foot and step to left side, quick (1 count).
3. Close right foot against left foot, transferring weight, quick (1 count).
4. Continuing to turn left, step forward on left foot, slow (2 counts).
5. Follow through with the right foot and step to right side, quick (1 count).
6. Close left foot against right foot, transferring weight, quick (1 count).

(You have now done a half turn. To complete the turn repeat 1 through 6.)

LEFT TURN
FOXTROT—CLOSED POSITION

5. Waltz

THE American waltz with its sentimental, romantic melodies is in a class by itself. It is outstanding on two counts—it is the oldest social dance done today and the only one in triple meter—3/4 ♩ ♩ ♩ time.

Because the American waltz is done slowly, it is not difficult for a beginner to practice to. And the simple 3/4 time will be found restful and easy. Listen for the three beats in each measure as you practice—the accent on the first beat—and cultivate a light, conservative style. After a while you will find the American waltz carrying you along with its easy rhythm and graceful, romantic melodies.

THE BASIC WALTZ FIGURE

Whether you are waltzing forward or backward or turning, you will be using part of or an entire figure called a square. (Starting and returning to the same place, a square includes four directions—forward, sideward, backward, and sideward.) See pages 46–47.

WALTZING FORWARD OR BACKWARD

Although the waltz consists basically of turns (squares done either to the left or right), we are going to learn the forward and backward half squares first.

Begin practicing a half square in the line of direction (forward for the man—backward for the woman). The figure requires one measure of music—3/4 ♩ ♩ ♩ time. Continuing in the line of direction, repeat the figure. Two half squares require two measures of music (six beats).

THE SQUARE

As soon as you have learned to waltz forward or backward you may progress to the square. A square requires two measures of music (six beats). The square *must* be memorized before you progress to the turns. And under no circumstances should you proceed to learn either the left or right turn until you have mastered the square.

TURNING

The square can be turned either to the left or to the right (the man and woman both turning left or right simultaneously). Four measures of music are required to complete the figure (twelve beats).

The feet, head, and arms follow in the direction of a turn, the chest, as usual initiating the lead. For example, if you are doing a left turn, the feet, head, and arms point in the left direction. Similarly, the feet, head, and arms point in a right direction if you are doing a right turn.

CHANGING DIRECTION

As soon as you have learned to turn either left or right, you may wish to change from one direction to another. The transition can be made quite easily by doing a half square.

If you have just completed a left turn and wish to progress to a right turn, do a half square (forward for the man—backward for the woman) in the line of direction so that your right foot (woman's left foot) will be released to begin a right turn.

To change from a right turn to a left turn do one half square in the line of direction and your left foot(woman's right foot) will be released to begin a left turn.

While you are practicing, keep on the balls of the feet—*at all times*. And for the follow-through principle in the waltz, watch for the dotted lines. *Most important.*

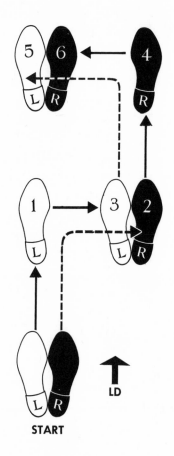

6. Close right foot against left foot, transferring weight (1 count).

5. Follow through with the left foot and step to left side (1 count).

4. Step forward on right foot (1 count).

3. Close left foot against right foot, transferring weight (1 count).

2. Follow through with the right foot and step to right side (1 count).

1. Step forward on left foot (1 count).

(Follow dotted line for follow-through.)

Man

*FORWARD HALF SQUARES
WALTZ–CLOSED POSITION*

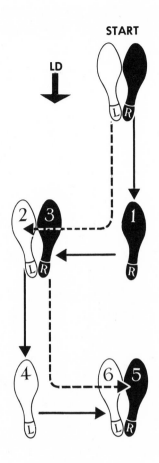

Woman

(Follow dotted line for follow-through.)

1. Step backward on right foot (1 count).

2. Follow through with the left foot and step to the left side (1 count).

3. Close right foot against left foot, transferring weight (1 count).

4. Step backward on left foot (1 count).

5. Follow through with the right foot and step to right side (1 count).

6. Close left foot against right foot, transferring weight (1 count).

BACKWARD HALF SQUARES
WALTZ—CLOSED POSITION

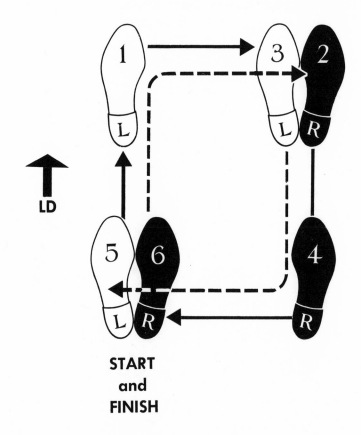

START
and
FINISH

6. Close right foot against left foot, transferring weight (1 count).

5. Follow through with the left foot and step to left side (1 count).

4. Step backward on right foot (1 count).

3. Close left foot against right foot, transferring weight (1 count).

2. Follow through with the right foot and step to right side (1 count).

1. Step forward on left foot (1 count).

(Follow dotted line for follow-through.)

Man

THE SQUARE
WALTZ–CLOSED POSITION

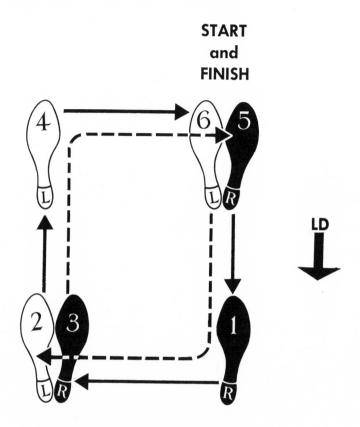

START
and
FINISH

Woman

(Follow dotted line for follow-through.)

1. Step backward on right foot (1 count).

2. Follow through with the left foot and step to the left side (1 count).

3. Close right foot against left foot, transferring weight (1 count).

4. Step forward on left foot (1 count).

5. Follow through with the right foot and step to right side (1 count).

6. Close left foot against right foot, transferring weight (1 count).

*THE SQUARE
WALTZ—CLOSED POSITION*

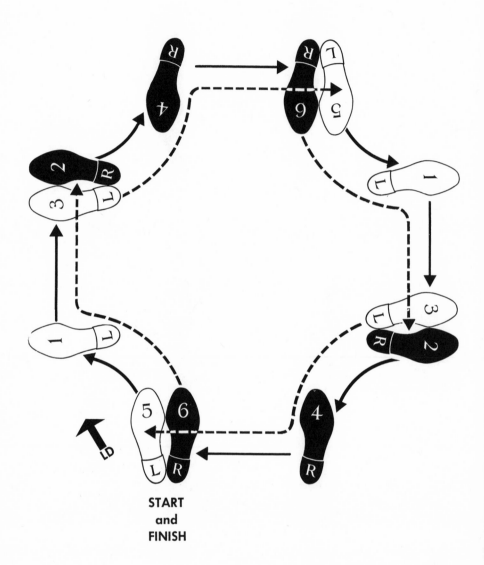

START
and
FINISH

Turn the book in your hand to correspond with the direction in which you are turning.

(You have now done a half turn. To complete the turn repeat 1 through 6.)

6. Close right foot against left foot, transferring weight (1 count).

5. Follow through with the left foot and step to left side (1 count).

4. Continuing to turn left, pulling the girl toward you, step backward on right foot (heel leading) (1 count).

3. Close left foot against right foot, transferring weight (1 count).

2. Follow through with the right foot and step to right side (1 count).

1. Chest lead, holding girl firmly with right hand while turning left, step forward on left foot (1 count).

(Follow dotted line for follow-through.)

Man

LEFT TURN
WALTZ—CLOSED POSITION

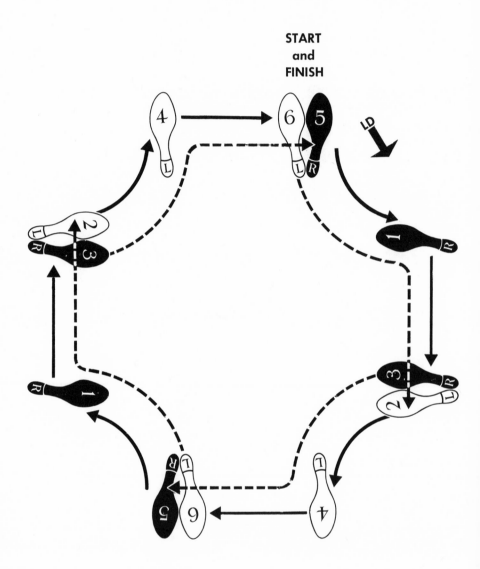

Turn the book in your hand to correspond with the direction in which you are turning.

Woman

(Follow dotted line for follow-through.)

1. Step backward on right foot (heel leading), chest turning left (1 count).

2. Follow through with the left foot and step to left side (1 count).

3. Close right foot against left foot, transferring weight (1 count).

4. Continuing to turn left, step forward on left foot (1 count).

5. Follow through with the right foot and step to right side (1 count).

6. Close left foot against right foot, transferring weight (1 count).

(You have now done a half turn. To complete the turn repeat 1 through 6.)

LEFT TURN
WALTZ—CLOSED POSITION

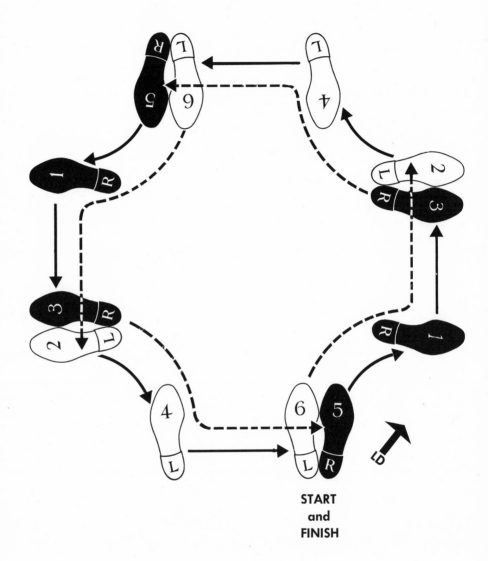

START
and
FINISH

Turn the book in your hand to correspond with the direction in which you are turning.

(You have now done a half turn. To complete the turn repeat 1 through 6.)

6. Close left foot against right foot, transferring weight (1 count).

5. Follow through with the right foot and step to the right side (1 count).

4. Continuing to turn right, pulling the girl toward you, step backward on left foot (heel leading) (1 count).

3. Close right foot against left foot, transferring weight (1 count).

2. Follow through with the left foot and step to the left side (1 count).

1. Chest lead, holding girl firmly with right hand while turning right, step forward on right foot (1 count).

(Follow dotted line for follow-through.)

Man

RIGHT TURN
WALTZ—CLOSED POSITION

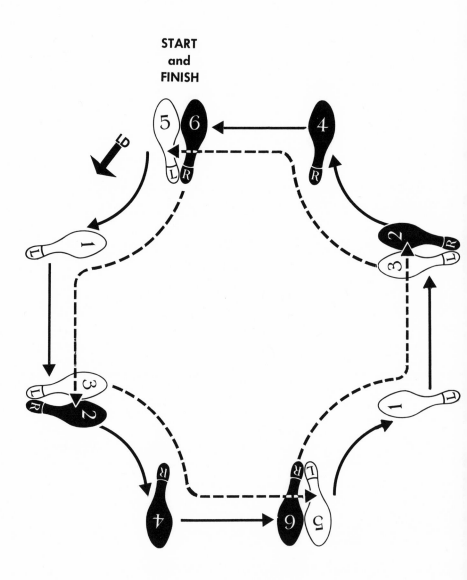

Turn the book in your hand to correspond with the direction in which you are turning.

Woman

(Follow dotted line for the follow-through.)

1. Step backward on left foot (heel leading), chest turning right (1 count).

2. Follow through with the right foot and step to right side (1 count).

3. Close left foot against right foot, transferring weight (1 count).

4. Continuing to turn right, step forward on right foot (1 count).

5. Follow through with the left foot and step to left side (1 count).

6. Close right foot against left foot, transferring weight (1 count).

(You have now done a half turn. To complete the turn repeat 1 through 6.)

RIGHT TURN
WALTZ—CLOSED POSITION

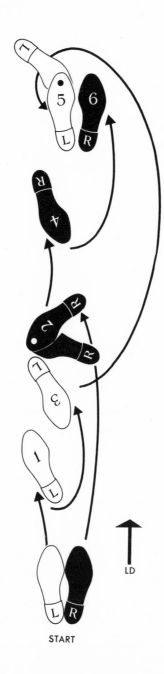

START

Turn the book in your hand to correspond with the direction in which you are turning.

(You have now completed another half turn and are facing in the line of direction.)

6. Close right foot to left foot, transferring the weight (1 count).

5. Stepping back on the left foot, pivot to the left (1 count).

4. Continuing to turn left, step back on the right foot (1 count).

(You have just completed a half turn and are now backing in the line of direction.)

3. Closing the left heel to the right toe, transfer the weight (1 count).

2. Step to the side on the right foot, pivoting a quarter turn to the left (1 count).

1. Step forward on left foot making a quarter turn to the left (1 count).

Facing in the line of direction, feet together, the weight over the ball of the right foot.

Man

**PROGRESSIVE
LEFT TURN
WALTZ—CLOSED
POSITION**

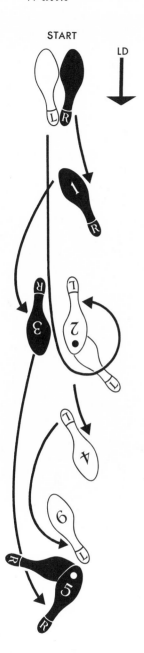

START

LD

Turn the book in your hand to correspond with the direction in which you are turning.

Woman

Backing in the line of direction, feet together, the weight over the ball of the left foot.

1. Step back on the right foot, making a quarter turn to the left (1 count).

2. Step back on the left foot, pivoting a quarter turn to the left (1 count).

3. Close right foot to left foot, transferring the weight (1 count).
    (You have just completed a half turn and are now facing in the line of direction.)

4. Continuing to turn left, step forward on the left foot (1 count).

5. Step to the side on the right foot, pivoting to the left (1 count).

6. Closing the left heel to the right toe, transfer the weight (1 count).
    (You have now completed another half turn and are backing in the line of direction.)

*PROGRESSIVE
LEFT TURN
WALTZ—CLOSED
POSITION*

START

Turn the book in your hand to correspond with the direction in which you are turning.

(You have now completed another half turn and are facing in the line of direction.)

6. Close left foot to right foot, transferring the weight (1 count).

5. Stepping back on the right foot, pivot to the right (1 count).

4. Continuing to turn right, step back on the left foot (1 count).

    (You have just completed a half turn and are now backing in the line of direction.)

3. Closing the right heel to the left toe, transfer the weight (1 count).

2. Step to the side on the left foot, pivoting a quarter turn to the right (1 count).

1. Step forward on right foot, making a quarter turn to the right (1 count).

    Facing in the line of direction, feet together, the weight over the ball of the left foot.

Man

PROGRESSIVE RIGHT TURN WALTZ—CLOSED POSITION

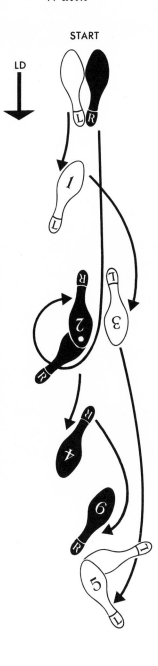

START

LD

Turn the book in your hand to correspond with the direction in which you are turning.

Woman

Backing in the line of direction, feet together, the weight over the ball of the right foot.

1. Step back on the left foot, making a quarter turn to the right (1 count).

2. Step back on the right foot, pivoting a quarter turn to the right (1 count).

3. Close left foot to right foot, transferring the weight (1 count).
(You have just completed a half turn and are now facing in the line of direction.)

4. Continuing to turn right, step forward on the right foot (1 count).

5. Step to the side on the left foot, pivoting to the right (1 count).

6. Closing the right heel to the left toe, transfer the weight (1 count).
(You have now completed another half turn and are backing in the line of direction.)

PROGRESSIVE RIGHT TURN WALTZ—CLOSED POSITION

THE BALANCE STEP

The balance step in the waltz consists of stepping and swaying forward, backward, or sideward. The step requires one measure of music (three beats). Here it is:

A step is taken on the first beat, held for the second and third beat—the active foot following through—as you rise on both toes.

There are various ways in which the balance step may be used. It may be done as a figure forward and back in place, and from side to side in place.

You will find the balance step especially useful in changing direction in the progressive turn. For example, if you have just completed a left turn and wish to progress to a right turn, do a balance step (forward for the man—backward for the woman) in the line of direction so that your right foot (woman's left foot) will be released to begin a right turn.

To change from a right turn to a left turn do a balance step in the line of direction and your left foot (woman's right foot) will be released to begin a left turn.

THE HESITATION

To add variety to your waltz, a figure called the hesitation may be used occasionally. The hesitation is a step-hold, requiring one measure of music (three beats). It consists of stepping in the line of direction on the first beat and holding for the second and third beats.

THE SERPENTINE

The serpentine figure consists of curving from side to side in the line of direction, moving from one step-out position to the other.

PRACTICING THE SERPENTINE

In order to acquire a smooth, continuous curve while practicing the serpentine, the man should exert a strong pressure through his right arm while maintaining a slight pressure of the left hand against the woman's right hand, the woman holding her right arm firm but not rigid. In addition, it will add much style to the figure if a light, swaying movement is maintained in the torso while pivoting and tilting.

In order to get into the serpentine figure, we suggest starting with a waltz square in closed position, using the second half of the square to get into left step-out position. To come out of the serpentine figure, a waltz square may be done in closed position.

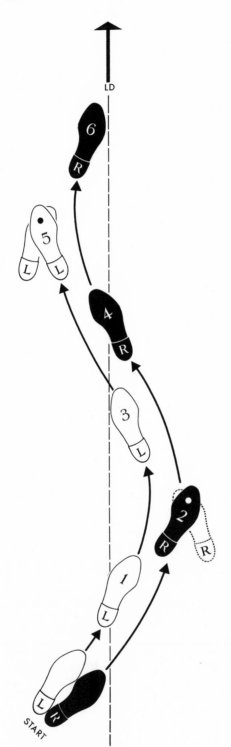

6. Continuing to tilt the woman to her left, step forward on the right foot, moving the woman from right step-out position to left step-out position (1 count).

5. Step forward on the left foot, pivoting to the right while tilting the woman to her left (1 count).

4. Step forward on the right foot (1 count).

(You are now facing diagonally left in the line of direction.)

3. Continuing to tilt the woman to her right, step forward on the left foot, moving the woman from left step-out position to right step-out position (1 count).

2. Step forward on the right foot, pivoting to left while tilting the woman to her right (1 count).

1. Step forward on the left foot (1 count).

Facing diagonally right in the line of direction in step-out position (left side to left side).

Man

WALTZ—
SERPENTINE

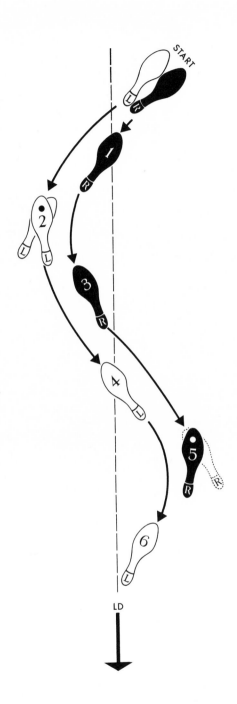

Woman

Backing diagonally right in the line of direction in step-out position (left side to left side).

1. Step back on the right foot (1 count).

2. Step back on the left foot, pivoting to the left, while tilting to the right (1 count).

3. Continuing to tilt to the right, step on the right foot, changing from left step-out position to right step-out position (1 count).
   (You are now backing diagonally left in the line of direction.)

4. Step back on the left foot (1 count).

5. Step back on the right foot, pivoting to the right and tilting to the left (1 count).

6. Continuing to tilt to the left, step back on the left foot, changing from right step-out position to left step-out position.

*WALTZ—
SERPENTINE*

6. Rumba

ALTHOUGH the rumba was at the height of its popularity several seasons ago, the dance is still a favorite of the all-around dancer.

The rumba, like the mambo, is essentially a "place" dance—a dance that is done pretty much in one spot. And each requires loose, relaxed knee work. The rumba, however, has its own characteristic rhythms and style. The delayed transference of weight in stepping, for instance, gives the rumba a unique appeal.

The music, however, will offer a greater challenge than the actual dance. But don't let the percussion instruments, with their syncopations and offbeats, throw you off. Listen for the insistent, steady beat of the claves, bongo drums, and maracas. And keep relaxed at all times while practicing this charming dance—the Cuban rumba.

BASIC RHYTHM

The Music

Like all the Latin-American dances, the Cuban rumba shows the influence of the Negroid and Spanish rhythms. And it is the blending of these rhythms that gives richness to the rumba music.

The music is in 4/4  time, the accents occurring on the first and third beats. Here is what a basic rumba beat is like:

$$\frac{4}{4}$$ ♩ ♩ ♩ |

Because of the variety of percussion instruments, the drums for example, it is easier to think of the standard Latin-American rhythm of eight beats in a measure. Here it is:

And just as "four beats ♩ ♩ ♩ ♩ in a bar" (measure) is typical of American jazz, the eight beats in a measure are typical of the rumba rhythm. The maracas (gourds shaken in the hands) will give you this rhythm. In dancing to the music, listen also for the claves and the bongo drums, which accent the rhythm. Both the claves (little sticks that are struck together) and the bongo drums beat out a typical Charleston beat. Here it is:

The Cuban rumba music is so relaxing, and the percussion instruments make the accents of the different rhythms so easy to listen to, that you should have no difficulty in keeping time.

The Step

The basic step of the rumba is done to music in 4/4
♩ ♩ ♩ ♩ time. The step consists of a quick, quick, slow.
Here is what the rhythm looks like:

QUICK   QUICK   SLOW

Two quick steps are taken to the side, followed by a slow step.
By repeating two quick steps to the side, followed by a slow
step we have completed a figure. Two measures of music in 4/4
time are required to complete the basic figure. Here is what we
have just described:

QUICK   QUICK   SLOW   QUICK   QUICK   SLOW

We are going to learn the following figures: the square in
closed position, the square turned to the left in closed position,
and the right turn-under break. Later we will describe the open
break, butterfly break, the crossover, and the spot turn.

THE RUMBA MOVEMENT

Before taking up the basic step (quick, quick, slow) we are
going to discuss the rhythm that underlies the steps.

In the progressive dances, for example, the waltz, the weight
of the body is transferred *as* the step is taken. In the rumba the
opposite is done—the weight *follows* the step. Actually, in the
rumba two movements are made on each step. The foot is placed
(no weight) on the floor, the weight following as the step is taken.

It is really quite simple. But make no mistake, the rumba requires plenty of practice. Therefore, the following section should be read and practiced carefully. Man or woman, stand with the feet together, the weight over the ball of the right foot.

Place (no weight) the left foot flat against the floor, slightly to the side, bending the left knee. Transfer the weight to the left foot, straightening the knee. (The right knee is now bent forward, no weight on the right foot.)

Place (no weight) the right foot flat against the floor, bending the right knee. Transfer the weight to the right foot, straightening the knee. (The left knee is now bent forward, no weight on the left foot.) Continuing, transfer the weight to the left foot, bending the right knee. Transfer the weight to the right foot, bending the left knee. Now, keeping the torso erect while practicing, repeat the movement until the rhythm becomes automatic, remembering always to place the foot before transferring the weight. That's all there is to the rumba movement!

Now that you have mastered the rumba movement in place, begin moving sidewards to the left, first placing and transferring the weight on the left foot, followed by placing and transferring the weight on the right foot. Do several steps in succession. Now practice moving sideward to the right, placing and transferring the weight on the right foot, and so forth. After you have become familiar with the steps moving sideward, practice moving forward and then backward, remembering to place the foot before transferring the weight. You are now ready to progress to the basic step.

THE BASIC STEP

The basic step consists of two quick steps and a slow step. It may be done in a square, a turn, and a break. When partners are in an open break the so-called Cuban walk is done to the same quick, quick, slow rhythm.

THE RUMBA SQUARE

Starting and returning to the same place, a square includes four directions—sideward, forward, sideward, and backward. See pages 70–71.

Begin practicing a half square in the line of direction (forward for the man—backward for the woman). The figure requires one measure of music in 4/4   time. Continuing with the second half of the square (backward for the man—forward for the woman), repeat the figure. (Two half squares require two measures of music, eight beats.) You have now done two basic steps in the quick, quick, slow rhythm. The square must be memorized before you progress to the left turn.

THE LEFT TURN SQUARE

The square can be turned to the left (the man and woman both turning to the left simultaneously). Four measures of music are required to complete the figure.

The feet, head, and arms follow in the direction of a turn, the chest as usual initiating the lead. For example, in doing the left turn, the feet, head, and arms point in the left direction.

THE BREAKS

The rumba, like the lindy, has many delightful breaks. We are going to start by learning the simplest break first.

The turn-under is based on the rumba square so it will be easy to learn this break. The man, however, should keep his left hand sufficiently relaxed so that the woman's fingers may pivot in

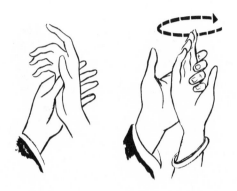

his easily, as she does the right turn-under with her right arm.

From here you may progress to the break in open position that is used in the Cuban walk. The butterfly breaks may follow or the crossover. Try them—they are delightful figures and will add much style to your rumba.

In all of the preceding breaks the right and left hand are used freely by the man in moving the woman from one position to another. Therefore, the leads will have to be given promptly and quickly. At all times, the elbows should be kept rather close to the body. And on the open breaks, the woman's arms should be bent at the elbows, the hands vertical, the fingers curving over naturally.

Now, you are ready to do these fascinating figures and breaks.

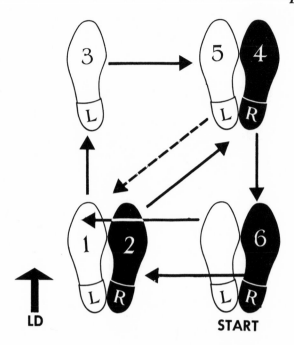

Man

1. Place the left foot to the left side, knee bent, no weight, quick (1 count).

2. Transferring the weight to the left foot, close the right foot to the left foot, right knee bent, no weight, quick (1 count).

3. Transferring the weight to the right foot, place the left foot forward, knee bent, no weight, slow (2 counts).

4. Transferring the weight to the left foot, place the right foot to the right side, knee bent, no weight, quick (1 count).

5. Transferring the weight to the right foot, close the left foot to the right foot, left knee bent, no weight, quick (1 count).

6. Transferring the weight to the left foot, place the right foot back, knee bent, no weight, slow (2 counts).

(To repeat the figure, transfer the weight to the right foot.)

THE SQUARE
RUMBA—CLOSED POSITION

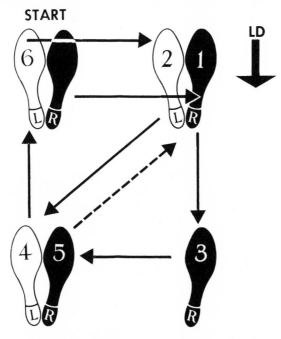

Woman

1. Place the right foot to the right side, knee bent, no weight, quick (1 count).

2. Transferring the weight to the right foot, close the left foot to the right foot, left knee bent, no weight, quick (1 count).

3. Transferring the weight to the left foot, place the right foot back, knee bent, no weight, slow (2 counts).

4. Transferring the weight to the right foot, place the left foot to the left side, knee bent, no weight, quick (1 count).

5. Transferring the weight to the left foot, close the right foot to the left foot, right knee bent, no weight, quick (1 count).

6. Transferring the weight to the right foot, place the left foot forward, knee bent, no weight, slow (2 counts).

(To repeat the figure, transfer the weight to the left foot.)

THE SQUARE
RUMBA—CLOSED POSITION

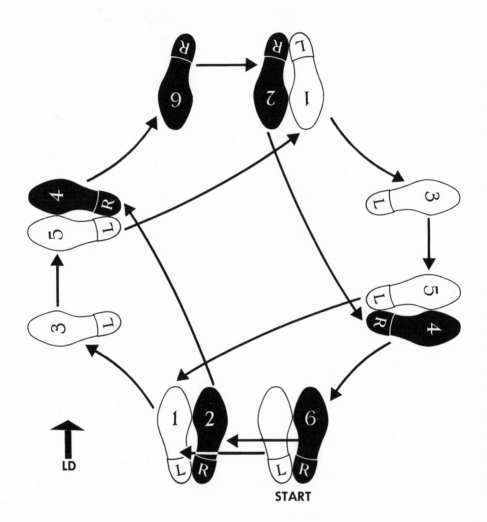

Turn the book in your hand to correspond with the direction in which you are turning.

Man

1. Place the left foot to the left side, knee bent, no weight, quick (1 count).

2. Transferring the weight to the left foot, close the right foot to the left foot, right knee bent, no weight, quick (1 count).

3. Transferring the weight to the right foot while turning to the left, place the left foot forward, knee bent, no weight, slow (2 counts).

4. Continuing to turn, transfer the weight to the left foot, placing the right foot to the right side, knee bent, no weight, quick (1 count).

5. Transferring the weight to the right foot, close the left foot to the right foot, left knee bent, no weight, quick (1 count).

6. Transferring the weight to the left foot while turning to the left, place the right foot back, knee bent, no weight, slow (2 counts).

(You have now done a half turn. To complete the turn, transfer the weight to the right foot, repeating 1 through 6.)

LEFT TURN
RUMBA–CLOSED POSITION

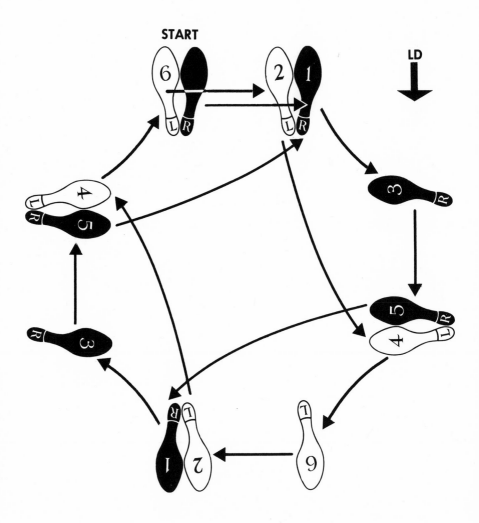

Turn the book in your hand to correspond with the direction in which you are turning.

Woman

1. Place the right foot to the right side, knee bent, no weight, quick (1 count).

2. Transferring the weight to the right foot, close the left foot to the right foot, left knee bent, no weight, quick (1 count).

3. Transferring the weight to the left foot while turning to the left, place the right foot back, knee bent, no weight, slow (2 counts).

4. Continuing to turn, transfer the weight to the right foot, placing the left foot to the left side, knee bent, no weight, quick (1 count).

5. Transferring the weight to the left foot, close the right foot to the left foot, right knee bent, no weight, quick (1 count).

6. Transferring the weight to the right foot while turning to the left, place the left foot forward, knee bent, no weight, slow (2 counts).

(You have now done a half turn. To complete the turn, transfer the weight to the left foot, repeating 1 through 6.)

LEFT TURN
RUMBA—CLOSED POSITION

THE RIGHT TURN-UNDER

Man

(The right turn-under break consists of the man turning the woman under her right arm, the woman walking in a circle close to the man and resuming the closed position.)

Facing in the line of direction, in closed position, feet together, the weight over the ball of the right foot.

1. Do a complete rumba square in the quick, quick, slow rhythm, raising the woman's right arm to prepare for the turn-under as you step back on the slow.

2. Continuing to do another rumba square, push the left side of the woman's torso firmly with your right hand, turning her under her right arm, resuming the closed position as you step back on the slow.

The right hand is released after the lead for the turn-under. The arms are lowered and the right hand placed under the woman's left shoulder blade as you resume the closed position.

THE RIGHT TURN-UNDER

Woman

(The right turn-under break consists of the woman turning under her right arm, walking in a circle close to the man and resuming the closed position.)

Backing in the line of direction, in closed position, feet together, the weight over the ball of the left foot.

1. Do a complete rumba square in the quick, quick, slow rhythm, raising the right arm to prepare for the turn-under as you step forward on the slow.

You are now going to describe a circle to the right as you turn under your arm.

2. Beginning with the right foot, take three steps forward in the quick, quick, slow rhythm, turning in front of the man, and continuing forward in a half square into closed position.

The left hand is released after the lead for the turn-under. The arms are lowered and the left hand placed on the man's right shoulder as you resume the closed position.

THE OPEN BREAK

The figure consists of the man and woman walking backward or forward in a circle maintaining the open break position. The open break position is obtained, from a closed position, by the man backing sideways away from the woman or pushing the woman sideways away from him. In addition, one can get into open break position by using a butterfly break, the right turn-under, or a half square. We are going to describe the figure starting from a square.

LEADING AND FOLLOWING

In the open break position the man holds the woman's right hand in his left hand in the rumba hand clasp. As he backs up, drawing the woman toward him, he will have to press down on the woman's wrist in order to control the direction in which they are moving. A strong left-hand lead will be necessary to reverse the turn. As the man moves forward, backing the woman, he increases the pressure of his left hand.

As the woman is drawn forward, it will be necessary for her to lean back slightly, bending the elbow, while keeping the right arm firm but not rigid. As the woman backs up in the reverse turn her right hand resists the pressure of the man's left hand.

At all times, the bodies must be kept in alignment while moving in the circle.

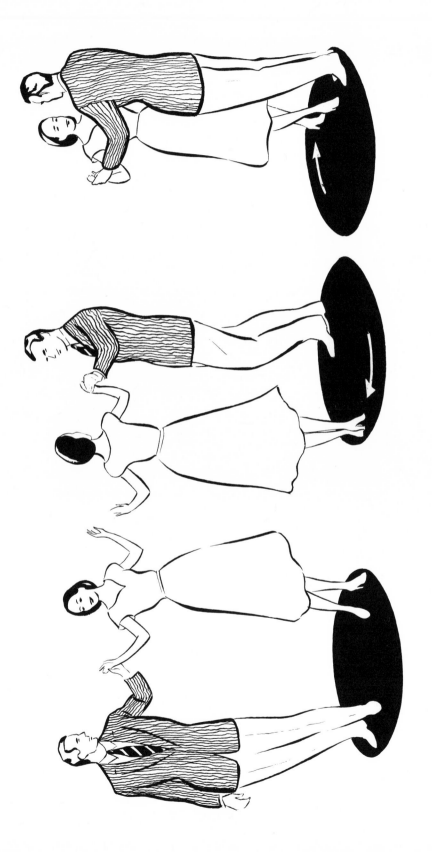

THE OPEN BREAK

Man

Standing in closed position, feet together, the weight over the right foot.

1. Step to the left side with the left foot, quick (1 count).

2. Close the right foot to the left foot, quick (1 count).

3. Pushing the woman away, step forward with the left foot, opening out to the right, slow (2 counts).

(You are now standing in the open break position, left arm extended in the rumba clasp, the right arm bent at the elbow.)

You are now going to back in a circle to the right as you pull the woman gradually toward you. (Keep shoulders parallel.)

4. Beginning with the right foot, take several steps backward in the quick, quick, slow rhythm (the Cuban walk) until you have brought the woman into closed position.

(The figure may be finished off by doing a square in place.)

Woman

Standing in closed position, feet together, the weight over the left foot.

1. Step to the right side with the right foot, quick (1 count).

2. Close the left foot to the right foot, quick (1 count).

3. Backing away from the man, step back on the right foot, opening out to the left, slow (2 counts).

(You are now standing in the open break position, your right hand in the man's left hand, your left arm bent at the elbow.)

You are now going to describe a circle to the right as the man pulls you toward him. (Keep shoulders parallel.)

4. Beginning with the left foot take several steps forward in the quick, quick, slow rhythm (the Cuban walk) until you are back in closed position.

(The figure may be finished off by doing a square in place.)

THE BUTTERFLY BREAKS

The butterfly breaks consist of the man and woman opening out and closing while pivoting on the supporting foot.

Man

Stand in closed position, feet together, the weight over the ball of the right foot.

The left butterfly:
1. Opening out to the left, step on the left foot, across and back of the right foot, while turning the woman out to the right, quick (1 count).
2. Closing in, step in place on the right foot, quick (1 count).
3. Resuming the closed position, step on the left foot, slow (2 counts).

The right butterfly:
1. Opening out to the right, step on the right foot, across and back of the left foot; turning the woman out to the left, release your right hand, quick (1 count).
2. Closing in, step in place on the left foot, quick (1 count).
3. Resuming the closed position, step on the right foot, placing the right hand under the woman's left shoulder blade, slow (2 counts).

Woman

Stand in closed position, feet together, the weight over the ball of the left foot.

The right butterfly:
1. Opening out to the right, step on the right foot, across and back of the left foot, quick (1 count).
2. Closing in, step in place on the left foot, quick (1 count).
3. Resuming the closed position, step on the right foot, slow (2 counts).

The left butterfly:
1. Opening out to the left, step on the left foot, across and back of the right foot, quick (1 count).
2. Closing in, step in place on the right foot, quick (1 count).
3. Resuming the closed position, step on the left foot, slow (2 counts).

RUMBA—CROSSOVER

Man

Standing in closed position, feet together, the weight over the right foot, holding the woman's right hand in your left hand.

Left crossover:

1. Pivoting on the right foot to the right, place the left foot across the right foot, knee bent, quick (1 count).

2. Transferring the weight to the left foot, bend the right knee in place, quick (1 count).

3. Transferring the weight to the right foot, pivot slightly to the left, closing the left foot to the right foot (left knee bent), slow (2 counts).

Right crossover, continuing:

1. Transfer the weight to the left foot, pivoting to the left, placing the right foot across the left foot, knee bent, quick (1 count).

2. Transferring the weight to the right foot, bend the left knee in place, quick (1 count).

3. Transferring the weight to the left foot, pivot slightly to the right, closing the right foot to the left foot (right knee bent), slow (2 counts).

(To repeat the figure, transfer the weight to the right foot.)

RUMBA—CROSSOVER

Woman

Standing in closed position, feet together, the weight over the left foot, the right hand held by the man's left hand.

Right crossover:

1. Pivoting on the left foot to the left, place the right foot across the left foot, knee bent, quick (1 count).

2. Transferring the weight to the right foot, bend the left knee in place, quick (1 count).

3. Transferring the weight to the left foot, pivot slightly to the right, closing the right foot to the left foot (right knee bent), slow (2 counts).

Left crossover, continuing:

1. Transfer the weight to the right foot, pivoting to the right, placing the left foot across the right foot, knee bent, quick (1 count).

2. Transferring the weight to the left foot, bend the right knee in place, quick (1 count).

3. Transferring the weight to the right foot, pivot slightly to the left, closing the left foot to the right foot (left knee bent), slow (2 counts).

(To repeat the figure, transfer the weight to the left foot.)

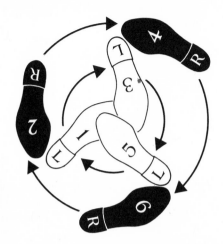

Turn the book in your hand to correspond with the direction in which you are turning.

Man

Stand in closed position, feet together, the weight over the ball of the right foot.

1. Turning slightly to the right, step to the side on the left foot, quick (1 count).

2. Continuing to the right, step on right foot in back of left heel, at right angle, quick (1 count).

3. Continuing to the right, step to the side on the left foot, slow (2 counts).

4. Continuing to the right, step on right foot in back of left heel, at right angle, quick (1 count).

5. Continuing to the right, step to the side with the left foot, quick (1 count).

6. Continuing to the right, step on right foot in back of left heel, at right angle, slow (2 counts).

RIGHT

RUMBA—SPOT TURN

Turn the book in your hand to correspond with the direction in which you are turning. (See also page 93.)

Woman

Stand in closed position, feet together, the weight over the ball of the left foot.

1. Step forward on the right foot turning slightly to the right, quick (1 count).

2. Continuing to turn right, step to the side with the left foot, quick (1 count).

3. Continuing to turn right, step on the right foot, right heel in front of left toe, at right angle, slow (2 counts).

4. Continuing to turn right, step to the side with the left foot, quick (1 count).

5. Continuing to turn right, step on the right foot, right heel in front of left toe, at right angle, quick (1 count).

6. Continuing to turn right, step to the side with the left foot, slow (2 counts).

RIGHT

RUMBA—SPOT TURN

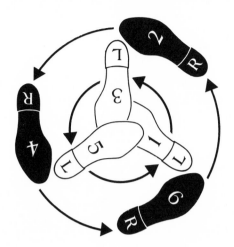

Turn the book in your hand to correspond with the direction in which you are turning. (See also page 96.)

Man

Stand in closed position, feet together, the weight over the ball of the right foot.

1. Turning to the left, step on the left foot, quick (1 count).

2. Continuing to the left, step to the side with the right foot, quick (1 count).

3. Continuing to the left, step on left foot in front of right toe, at right angle, slow (2 counts).

4. Continuing to the left, step to the side on the right foot, quick (1 count).

5. Continuing to the left, step on left foot in front of right toe, at right angle, quick (1 count).

6. Continuing to the left, step to the side on the right foot, slow (2 counts).

LEFT

RUMBA—SPOT TURN

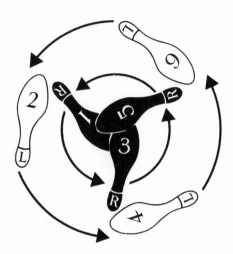

Turn the book in your hand to correspond with the direction in which you are turning.

Woman

Stand in closed position, feet together, the weight over the ball of the left foot.

1. Step to the side on the right foot, turning slightly to the left, quick (1 count).

2. Continuing to turn left, step on left foot in back of right heel, at right angle, quick (1 count).

3. Continuing to turn left, step on right foot to the side, slow (2 counts).

4. Continuing to turn left, step on left foot in back of right heel, at right angle, quick (1 count).

5. Continuing to turn left, step to the side with the right foot, quick (1 count).

6. Continuing to turn left, step on left foot in back of right heel, at right angle, slow (2 counts).

LEFT

RUMBA–SPOT TURN

Sl OT TURN

We have described the spot turn to the right, followed by the spot turn to the left. It is not necessary, however, to follow this sequence. Either of the spot turns may be followed, for variety, by a butterfly break or a square.

In order to break from a right spot turn the man must have his left foot free (right foot for the woman). To break from a left spot turn the man must have his right foot free (left foot for the woman).

PRACTICING THE SPOT TURN

Having learned the spot turn you are now ready to practice with a partner. You will find it quite easy to get into the figure, starting from a square—turning slightly to the right on the second half of the square.

Chests must be kept *parallel* at all times, the woman keeping her foot between the man's feet while practicing the turn. In addition, the woman can facilitate the man's lead for the turn by leaning away slightly while maintaining a slight pressure of the left hand against the man's right shoulder. In order to reverse a spot turn, the man will have to exert a *strong* pressure with his right hand.

VARIATIONS

As has already been indicated, there is nothing set about the progression of one figure to another. The preceding figures and breaks, therefore, may be varied at will. For example, on the right turn-under the man may turn under his left arm as the woman turns under her right arm. And the sequence of moving forward and backward may be varied at any time—in either closed position or open break position. Eventually you will find yourself doing all sorts of new combinations. And try some fast rumbas!

7. The Mambo

THE mambo, more popular than ever, is an offbeat dance of Cuban origin. Like the rumba, the mambo can be done in a conservative style or with the greatest freedom—in closed position and in open breaks.

The music, with its conga drums, offbeats, and riffs is fascinating and offers endless possibilities for new combinations of steps.

THE BASIC RHYTHM

The music of the mambo is in 4/4 ♩ ♩ ♩ ♩ time, the accents of the basic mambo rhythm occurring on the first beat and second half of the second beat. Here is what a typical mambo rhythm looks like:

As you can see the syncopation results in a jerky, staccato rhythm.

THE BASIC STEP

The basic step of the mambo is done in 4/4 ♩ ♩ ♩ ♩ time. The basic rhythm is slow, quick, quick. Here it is:

SLOW   QUICK   QUICK

In dancing the mambo step the feet are brought together on the fourth beat and held together through the first beat, followed by a break (stepping forward, backward, or sideward) on the second beat, and stepping in place on the third beat. Here it is:

HOLD   STEP   STEP

(BREAK)

The basic step requires one measure of music. The step is repeated, requiring two measures of music. And here it is:

HOLD   STEP   STEP   HOLD   STEP   STEP

(BREAK)   (BREAK)

We are going to learn the basic step forward and back and to the side. From here we will progress to the crossover, the right turn-under, and the charge. Each figure will be described. Some mention will be made of the walk-around turns and variations of all these figures in closed position and in the open break.

And for those who are really good, we will describe the chase, the coil turn, and the latest dance—the cha cha cha.

We are now ready to proceed with the mambo.

PRACTICING THE MAMBO

It is customary to start practicing a dance from a position with the feet together. The mambo, however, starts from a position with the feet apart. Therefore, it will be necessary to take a preparatory figure on the first beat of the music in order to begin the mambo correctly. The preparatory figure will also enable you to begin the dance on the mambo beat, which is the fourth beat of the measure.

PREPARATORY FIGURE

Man

Stand with feet together, the weight over the ball of the right foot.

1. Step to the left side with the left foot, quick (1 count).
2. Step back on the right foot, quick (1 count).
3. Step forward on the left foot, quick (1 count).
   Here is what the transition into the mambo beat looks like:

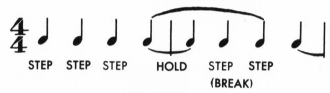

STEP   STEP   STEP   HOLD   STEP   STEP

(BREAK)

MAMBO
BASIC STEP

Man

Forward basic step:

1. Close the right foot to the left foot, knee bent (no weight).
   Transfer the weight to the right foot, straightening the knee, left knee bends. — Slow (2 counts)
2. Step forward on the left foot, quick (1 count).
3. Step in place on the right foot, quick (1 count).

Backward basic step:

1. Close the left foot to the right foot, knee bent (no weight).
   Transfer the weight to the left foot, straightening the knee, right knee bends. — Slow (2 counts)
2. Step back with the right foot, quick (1 count).
3. Step in place on the left foot, quick (1 count).

Now practice the basic step, without looking at the directions, calling out, "Slow, quick, quick," as you practice, remembering to close-hold on "slow," break on "quick," and step in place on "quick."

PREPARATORY FIGURE

Woman

Stand with feet together, the weight over the ball of the left foot.

1. Step to the right side with the right foot, quick (1 count).

2. Step forward on the left foot, quick (1 count).

3. Step back on the right foot, quick (1 count).

BASIC STEP

Woman

Backward basic step:

1. Close the left foot to the right foot, knee bent (no weight).
    Transfer the weight to the left foot, straightening the knee, right knee bends. — Slow (2 counts)

2. Step back with the right foot, quick (1 count).

3. Step in place on the left foot, quick (1 count).

Forward basic step:

1. Close the right foot to the left foot, knee bent (no weight).
    Transfer the weight to the right foot, straightening the knee, left knee bends. — Slow (2 counts)

2. Step forward on the left foot, quick (1 count).

3. Step in place on the right foot, quick (1 count).

Now practice the basic step, without looking at the directions, calling out, "Slow, quick, quick," as you practice, remembering to close-hold on "slow," break on "quick," and step in place on "quick."

SIDEWARD BASIC STEP

Man

Left side:

1. Close the right foot to the left foot, knee bent (no weight).
   Transfer the weight to the right foot, straightening the knee, left knee bends. — Slow (2 counts)
2. Step to the left side on the left foot, quick (1 count).
3. Step in place on the right foot, quick (1 count).

Right side:

1. Close the left foot to the right foot, knee bent (no weight).
   Transfer the weight to the left foot, straightening the knee, right knee bends. — Slow (2 counts)
2. Step to the right side on the right foot, quick (1 count).
3. Step in place on the left foot, quick (1 count).

SIDEWARD BASIC STEP

Woman

Right side:

1. Close the left foot to the right foot, knee bent (no weight).
   Transfer the weight to the left foot, straightening the knee, right knee bends. — Slow (2 counts)
2. Step to the right side on the right foot, quick (1 count).
3. Step in place on the left foot, quick (1 count).

Left side:

1. Close the right foot to the left foot, knee bent (no weight).
   Transfer the weight to the right foot, straightening the knee, left knee bends. — Slow (2 counts)
2. Step to the left side on the left foot, quick (1 count).
3. Step in place on the right foot, quick (1 count).

CROSSOVER

Man

Starting position, facing your partner, weight over left foot, holding the woman's right hand in your left hand.

Left crossover:

1. Close the right foot to the left foot, knee bent. Transferring the weight to the right foot, pivot to the right. } Slow (2 counts)

2. Step with the left foot across the right foot, quick (1 count).

3. Step in place with the right foot, releasing the woman's right hand, quick (1 count).

Right crossover:

1. Taking the woman's left hand in your right hand, close the left foot to the right foot, knee bent. Transferring the weight to the left foot, pivot to the left. } Slow (2 counts)

2. Step with the right foot across the left foot, quick (1 count).

3. Step in place with the left foot, releasing the woman's left hand, quick (1 count).

(NOTE: In changing hands from one crossover to the other, the leads will have to be given promptly and quickly.)

CROSSOVER

Woman

Starting position, facing your partner, weight over right foot, the right hand held by the man's left hand.

Right crossover:

1. Close the left foot to the right foot, knee bent. Transferring the weight to the left foot, pivot to the left. — Slow (2 counts)

2. Step with the right foot across the left foot, quick (1 count).

3. Step in place with the left foot, releasing the man's left hand, quick (1 count).

Left crossover:

1. Placing your left hand in the man's right hand, close the right foot to the left foot, knee bent. Transferring the weight to the right foot, pivot to the right. — Slow (2 counts)

2. Step with the left foot across the right foot, quick (1 count).

3. Step in place with the right foot, releasing the man's right hand, quick (1 count).

RIGHT TURN-UNDER

Man

The right turn-under break consists of the man turning the woman under her right arm, the woman walking in a circle close to the man and resuming the closed position.

Stand in closed position, feet together, the weight over the left foot.

1. Do a forward basic step in the slow, quick, quick rhythm, raising the woman's right arm to prepare for the turn-under as you step back in place on the quick.

2. Continuing with a backward basic step, push the left side of the woman's torso firmly with your right hand, turning her under her right arm; lower the woman's right arm as you step forward in place on the quick.

The arms are lowered and the right hand placed under the woman's left shoulder blade as you resume the closed position.

 The man, however, should keep his left hand sufficiently relaxed so that the woman's fingers may pivot in his easily, as she does the right turn-under with her right arm.

RIGHT TURN-UNDER

Woman

The right turn-under break consists of the woman turning under her right arm, walking in a circle close to the man, and resuming the closed position.

Stand in closed position, feet together, the weight over the right foot.

1. Do a backward basic step in the slow, quick, quick rhythm, raising the right arm to prepare for the turn-under as you step forward in place on the quick.

You are now going to describe a circle to the right as you turn under your arm.

2. Beginning with the right foot, take three steps forward in the slow, quick, quick rhythm, turning in front of the man; lowering your right arm as you step in place on the right foot.

The arms are lowered and the left hand placed on the man's right shoulder as you resume the closed position.

THE CHARGE

Man

Starting position, facing partner, weight over left foot.

Left charge:

1. Close the right foot to the left foot, knee bent. Transferring the weight to the right foot, pivot a quarter turn to the right away from your partner.　　Slow (2 counts)

2. Stepping to the side with the left foot, thrust the left shoulder toward the woman's right shoulder, quick (1 count).

3. Step in place with the right foot, quick (1 count).

Right charge:

1. Close the left foot to the right foot, knee bent. Transferring the weight to the left foot, pivot a half turn to the left.　　Slow (2 counts)

2. Stepping to the side with the right foot, thrust the right shoulder toward the woman's left shoulder, quick (1 count).

3. Step in place with the left foot, quick (1 count).

To repeat the figure, a half turn is taken before each charge.

THE CHARGE

Woman

Starting position, facing partner, weight over right foot.

Right charge:

1. Close the left foot to the right foot, knee bent.┐
   Transferring the weight to the left foot, pivot │   Slow
   a quarter turn to the left away from your part- ├ (2 counts)
   ner.   ┘

2. Stepping to the side with the right foot, thrust the right shoulder toward the man's left shoulder, quick (1 count).

3. Step in place with the left foot, quick (1 count).

Left charge:

1. Close the right foot to the left foot, knee bent.┐   Slow
   Transferring the weight to the right foot, pivot ├ (2 counts)
   a half turn to the right.   ┘

2. Stepping to the side with the left foot, thrust the left shoulder toward the man's right shoulder, quick (1 count).

3. Step in place with the right foot, quick (1 count).

To repeat the figure, a half turn is taken before each charge.

THE CHASE

In the chase the man turns away from the woman, and she follows him. As the woman turns away from the man, he follows her. Partners continue chasing each other by taking half right and left turns alternately.

Man

Starting position, facing your partner, weight over left foot.

Right turn:

1. Place the right foot slightly ahead of the left foot.
Transfer the weight to the right foot. — Slow (2 counts)

2. Step forward with the left foot, pivoting to the right, quick (1 count).

3. Continuing to pivot to the right, step in place with the right foot, quick (1 count).

You have now done one half-right turn.

Left turn:

1. Place the left foot slightly ahead of the right foot.
Transfer the weight to the left foot. — Slow (2 counts)

2. Step forward with the right foot, pivoting to the left, quick (1 count).

3. Continuing to pivot to the left, step in place with the left foot, quick (1 count).

You have now done one half-left turn.

The turns may be repeated several times. To resume the original position (facing your partner) it will be necessary for the man to do a basic step in place while the woman completes her last turn.

THE CHASE

Woman

It will be necessary for the woman to do a backward basic step in place while the man executes the right turn.

Starting position, facing your partner, weight over right foot.

Backward basic step:

1. Close the left foot to the right foot.   ⎞   Slow
    Transfer the weight to the left foot.   ⎠   (2 counts)

2. Step back with the right foot, quick (1 count).

3. Step in place with the left foot, quick (1 count).

Right turn:

1. Place the right foot slightly ahead of the left ⎞
    foot.   ⎬   Slow
    Transfer the weight to the right foot.   ⎠ (2 counts)

2. Step forward with the left foot, pivoting to the right, quick (1 count).

3. Continuing to pivot to the right, step in place with the right foot, quick (1 count).

You have now done one half-right turn.

Left turn:

1. Place the left foot slightly ahead of the right ⎞
    foot.   ⎬   Slow
    Transfer the weight to the left foot.   ⎠ (2 counts)

2. Step forward with the right foot, pivoting to the left, quick (1 count).

3. Continuing to pivot to the left, step in place with the left foot, quick (1 count).

You have now done one half-left turn.

COIL TURN

Holding the woman's left hand in his right hand, the man coils the woman into his right arm, the woman taking a half-left turn, followed by the man uncoiling the woman as she takes a half-right turn.

Man

Starting position, facing your partner, weight over left foot, holding the woman's right hand in your left hand.

1. Closing the right foot to the left foot, the man takes the woman's left hand in his right hand. Transfer the weight to the right foot. } Slow (2 counts)

2. Still holding both hands, step back with the left foot, quick (1 count).

3. Step in place with the right foot, pulling the woman into your right arm with left hand, releasing the woman's right hand, quick (1 count).

4. Still holding the woman over your right arm, close the left foot to the right foot. Transfer the weight to the left foot. } Slow (2 counts)

5. Step back with the right foot, quick (1 count).

6. Step in place with the left foot, uncoiling the woman with your right hand, quick (1 count).

7. Continuing to uncoil the woman, close the right foot to the left foot. Transfer the weight to the right foot, taking the woman's right hand in your left hand. } Slow (2 counts)

The figure, coiling and uncoiling, may now be repeated by returning to number two (stepping back with the left foot).

COIL TURN

Woman

Starting position, facing your partner, weight over right foot, the right hand held by the man's left hand.

1. Close the left foot to the right foot, as the man takes your left hand in his right hand.
   Transfer the weight to the left foot. } Slow (2 counts)

2. Still holding both hands, step back with the right foot, quick (1 count).

3. Step forward with the left foot, making one quarter-left turn into the man's right arm, releasing the man's left hand, quick (1 count).

4. Continuing to turn left into man's right arm, close the right foot to the left foot.
   Transfer the weight to the right foot. } Slow (2 counts)

5. Step back with the left foot, quick (1 count).

6. Uncoiling from man's right arm, step forward with the right foot, making one quarter turn to the right, quick (1 count).

7. Continuing to uncoil from man's right arm, close the left foot to the right foot.
   Transfer the weight to the left foot, placing your right hand in the man's left hand. } Slow (2 counts)

The figure, coiling and uncoiling, may now be repeated by returning to number two (stepping back with the right foot).

PRACTICE

Having learned the basic step forward and backward and sideward, you are now ready to dance with a partner in the customary closed position. From the closed position you may progress to an open break. The man pushes the woman away on the forward basic step, continuing to separate on the backward basic step. From this position the crossover, the charge, or the chase may be done.

VARIATIONS

Occasionally you may wish to vary the sequence of the preceding figures. For example, the forward basic step may be done twice consecutively in an open break by both the man and woman —and similarly, the back basic step. Instead of doing the side basic step consecutively, however, you may vary the figure by doing one side basic, followed by a charge. The crossover can be made more interesting by using one crossover and one basic step. When the left crossover is used, you break back on the basic step. When the right crossover is used, you break forward on the basic step. The transition from the left crossover to the right crossover may be done by using a forward basic step.

In addition, the mambo walk-around turns may be done from a basic step—the man turning to the left while the woman turns to the right; partners walk around in a circle to the slow, quick, quick rhythm while making a complete turn. The figure may be finished with a basic step.

CHA CHA CHA

Now that you have mastered the mambo, try the cha cha cha. It is the latest dance step being done to mambo music and the easiest to execute. The cha cha cha has a light, bouncy rhythm that appeals to all ages.

THE BASIC RHYTHM

The music is in 4/4  time, the accent occurring on the first beat and the secondary accent on the third beat. Here it is:

THE BASIC STEP

In dancing the cha cha cha three steps are taken in place (a "ball change," transferring the weight quickly from one foot to the other) on the fourth and first beats of the music, followed by a break (stepping forward or backward) on the second beat, and stepping in place on the third beat. Here it is:

STEP   STEP   STEP   STEP   STEP

As you can see, the cha cha cha step begins on the mambo beat—the fourth beat of the music. And since you are already familiar with the mambo rhythm, you will find it quite easy to learn the cha cha cha.

We are going to learn the basic step forward and backward and sideward, the crossover, and the chase. Later we will describe the cha cha hop.

And remember—for those who really get wound up—any of the preceding mambo figures or breaks may be done in the cha cha cha rhythm: the right turn-under, the walk-around turns, and the coil turn.

THE BASIC STEP

Man

Starting position, facing your partner, weight over left foot.

Forward basic step:

1. Step in place three times, beginning with the right foot (right, left, right, 2 counts).

2. Step forward on the left foot (1 count).

3. Step in place on the right foot (1 count).

Backward basic step:

1. Step in place three times, beginning with the left foot (left, right, left, 2 counts).

2. Step back with the right foot (1 count).

3. Step in place on the left foot (1 count).

THE BASIC STEP

Woman

Starting position, facing your partner, weight over right foot.

Backward basic step:

1. Step in place three times, beginning with the left foot (left, right, left, 2 counts).

2. Step back with the right foot (1 count).

3. Step in place on the left foot (1 count).

Forward basic step:

1. Step in place three times, beginning with the right foot (right, left, right, 2 counts).

2. Step forward on the left foot (1 count).

3. Step in place on the right foot (1 count).

SIDEWARD BASIC STEP

Man

Starting position, facing your partner, weight over left foot.

Left side:

1. Step in place three times, beginning with the right foot (right, left, right, 2 counts).

2. Step to the left side on the left foot, quick (1 count).

3. Step in place on the right foot, quick (1 count).

Right side:

1. Step in place three times, beginning with the left foot (left, right, left, 2 counts).

2. Step to the right side on the right foot, quick (1 count).

3. Step in place on the left foot, quick (1 count).

SIDEWARD BASIC STEP

Woman

Starting position, facing your partner, weight over right foot.

Right side:

1. Step in place three times, beginning with the left foot (left, right, left, 2 counts).

2. Step to the right side on the right foot, quick (1 count).

3. Step in place on the left foot, quick (1 count).

Left side:

1. Step in place three times, beginning with the right foot (right, left, right, 2 counts).

2. Step to the left side on the left foot, quick (1 count).

3. Step in place on the right foot, quick (1 count).

CROSSOVER

Man

Starting position, facing your partner, weight over left foot.

Left crossover:

1. Step in place three times, beginning with the right foot (right, left, right, 2 counts).
2. Pivoting on the right foot to the right, step with the left foot across the right foot (1 count).
3. Step in place with the right foot (1 count).

Right crossover:

1. Step in place three times, beginning with the left foot (left, right, left, 2 counts).
2. Pivoting on the left foot to the left, step with the right foot across the left foot (1 count).
3. Step in place with the left foot (1 count).

CROSSOVER

Woman

Starting position, facing your partner, weight over right foot.

Right crossover:

1. Step in place three times, beginning with the left foot (left, right, left, 2 counts).
2. Pivoting on the left foot to the left, step with the right foot across the left foot (1 count).
3. Step in place with the left foot (1 count).

Left crossover:

1. Step in place three times, beginning with the right foot (right, left, right, 2 counts).
2. Pivoting on the right foot to the right, step with the left foot across the right foot (1 count).
3. Step in place with the right foot (1 count).

THE CHASE

Man

Starting position, facing your partner, weight over left foot.

Right turn:

1. Step in place three times, beginning with the right foot (right, left, right, 2 counts).

2. Step forward on the left foot, pivoting to the right (1 count).

3. Continuing to pivot to the right, step in place on the right foot (1 count).

You have now done a half turn.

Left turn:

1. Step in place three times, beginning with the left foot (left, right, left, 2 counts).

2. Step forward on the right foot, pivoting to the left (1 count).

3. Continuing to pivot to the left, step in place on the left foot (1 count).

You have now done a half turn.

The turns may be repeated several times. To resume the original position (facing your partner) it will be necessary for the man to do a basic step in place while the woman completes her last turn.

THE CHASE

Woman

It will be necessary for the woman to do a backward basic step in place while the man executes the right turn.

Starting position, facing your partner, weight over right foot.

Backward basic step:

1. Step in place three times, beginning with the left foot (left, right, left, 2 counts).

2. Step back with the right foot (1 count).

3. Step in place with the left foot (1 count).

Right turn:

1. Step in place three times, beginning with the right foot (right, left, right, 2 counts).

2. Step forward on the left foot, pivoting to the right (1 count).

3. Continuing to pivot to the right, step in place on the right foot (1 count).

You have now done a half turn.

Left turn:

1. Step in place three times, beginning with the left foot (left, right, left, 2 counts).

2. Step forward on the right foot, pivoting to the left (1 count).

3. Continuing to pivot to the left, step in place on the left foot (1 count).

You have now done a half turn.

CHA CHA HOP

Want to really dress up the cha cha cha? Then try the cha cha hop. The figure consists of the man or woman stepping forward on the left foot, back in place on the right foot, hopping in place on the right foot, followed by three steps backward (left, right, left). The cha cha hop is followed by a basic step in place. Man or woman, step back on the right foot, step in place on the left foot, step in place three times (right, left, right).

Since the cha cha hop is done alternately by partners (facing each other), it will be necessary for the woman to do a basic step in place while the man does the hop. The man in turn does a basic step in place as the woman does the hop.

In order to do the cha cha hop on the mambo beat it will be necessary to do three steps in place on the fourth and first beats of the music, stepping forward on the second beat, followed by stepping back in place and hopping on the third beat. From here, you are on your own.

8. Tango

FOR something different try a tango! Its smooth, sleek style will add much to your social dancing—particularly the American fox-trot. The music is less complex than the rumba; and since the Argentine tango is done moderately slow, you will not find practice too difficult.

The lovely, plaintive melodies of the tango are most appealing and the strongly accented base in the music will help you keep time.

Long, smooth steps should be taken to maintain that sleek look so characteristic of the Argentine tango.

BASIC RHYTHM

The basic rhythm of the tango is slow, slow, quick-quick, slow. Two measures of music in 4/4 ♩ ♩ ♩ ♩ time are required to complete the rhythm. Here is what it looks like:

Two slow steps are taken followed by two quick steps and a slow step, at the end of which figure, the feet are brought together to form an arch. (Arching consists of drawing the foot slowly to the arch of the supporting foot, the weight remaining on the supporting foot.) By merely changing one's direction or position any number of fascinating combinations can be devised.

We are starting off with the more basic figures, the closed position, the dip, the step-out position, and promenade. Later we will go on to the crisscross and the run-around. Each of these figures is described.

PRACTICE

In learning the figures, start off with the closed position and progress to the dip. The step-out figure may follow. After you have practiced the individual figures you can begin to combine them. Progressing from the closed position to the dip, and on to the step-out position will be quite simple since you are already in the closed position at the end of each figure.

From here, you may progress to the promenade. The transition to the promenade can be made by pivoting in the line of direction on the last slow of the preceding figure. You will then be in the open position to begin the promenade. For variety, you might try the turn-under (promenade) figure in which the woman pivots in place to the right, the man continuing in the line of direction. For something tricky, try either the push-away break or the run-around.

And remember to try some new figures of your own.

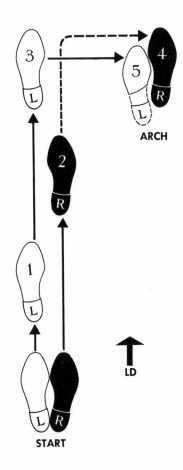

5. Draw the left foot slowly to the arch of the right foot, weight remaining on the right foot, slow (2 counts).

4. Follow through with the right foot and step to the right side, quick (1 count).

3. Step forward on the left foot, quick (1 count).

2. Step forward on the right foot, the left toe remaining in place, slow (2 counts).

1. Step forward in the line of direction on the left foot, the right toe remaining in place, slow (2 counts).

Man

TANGO—CLOSED POSITION

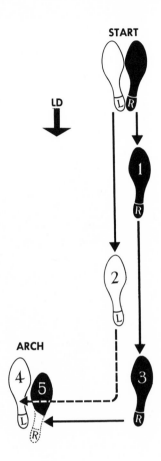

Woman

1. Step backward in the line of direction on the right foot, the left toe remaining in place, slow (2 counts).

2. Step backward on the left foot, the right toe remaining in place, slow (2 counts).

3. Step backward on the right foot, quick (1 count).

4. Follow through with the left foot and step to the left side, quick (1 count).

5. Draw the right foot slowly to the arch of the left foot, weight remaining on the left foot, slow (2 counts).

TANGO—CLOSED POSITION

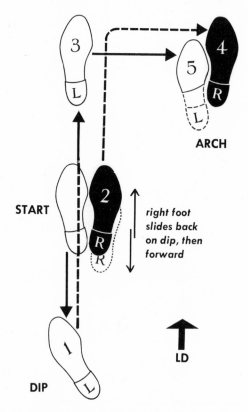

5. Draw the left foot slowly to the arch of the right foot, weight
    remaining on the right foot, slow (2 counts).

4. Follow through with the right foot and step to the right side,
    quick (1 count).

3. Step forward on the left foot, quick (1 count).

2. Step forward on the right foot, the left toe remaining in place,
    slow (2 counts).

1. Step back on the left foot, bending at the knee, right leg ex-
    tended slow (2 counts).

Man

DIP

TANGO—CLOSED POSITION

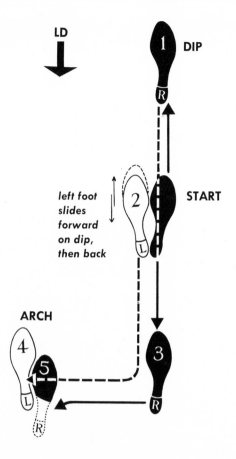

Woman

1. Step forward on the right foot, bending at the knee, left leg extended, toe remaining in place, slow (2 counts).

2. Step back on the left foot, slow (2 counts).

3. Step backward on the right foot, quick (1 count).

4. Follow through with the left foot and step to the left side, quick (1 count).

5. Draw the right foot slowly to the arch of the left foot, weight remaining on the left foot, slow (2 counts).

DIP

TANGO—CLOSED POSITION

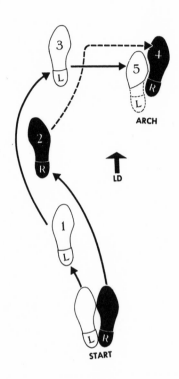

5. Draw the left foot slowly to the arch of the right foot, weight remaining on the right foot, slow (2 counts).

4. Follow through with the right foot and step to the right side, quick (1 count).

3. Following through, step forward and across with the left foot into closed position, quick (1 count).

2. Step forward and across with the right foot, slow (2 counts). You are now in step-out position.

1. Facing in the line of direction, in closed position, step diagonally forward on the left foot, the right toe remaining in place, slow (2 counts).

Man

TANGO—STEP-OUT POSITION

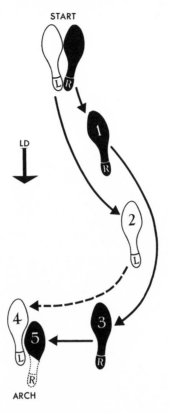

Woman

1. Backing in the line of direction, in closed position, step diagonally backward on the right foot, the left toe remaining in place, slow (2 counts).

2. Step in back of and across with the left foot, slow (2 counts). You are now in step-out position.

3. Following through, step back and across with the right foot, quick (1 count). You are now in closed position.

4. Follow through with the left foot and step to the left side, quick (1 count).

5. Draw the right foot slowly to the arch of the left foot, weight remaining on the left foot, slow (2 counts).

TANGO—STEP-OUT POSITION

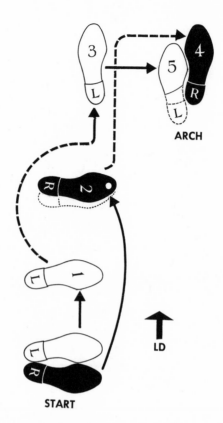

5. Draw the left foot slowly to the arch of the right foot, weight remaining on the right foot, slow (2 counts).

4. Follow through with the right foot and step to the right side, quick (1 count).

3. Step forward on the left foot, quick (1 count).

2. Step across in front of the left foot with right foot, swinging the girl into closed position in the line of direction, slow (2 counts).

1. Facing in the line of direction, in promenade position, step sideways on left foot, the right toe remaining in place, slow (2 counts).

Man

TANGO PROMENADE

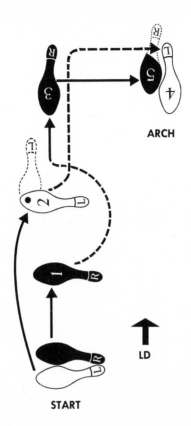

ARCH

LD

START

Woman

1. Facing in the line of direction, in promenade position, step sideways on right foot, the left toe remaining in place, slow (2 counts).

2. Step across in front of the right foot with left foot, pivoting into closed position, slow (2 counts).

3. Backing in the line of direction, step back on the right foot, quick (1 count).

4. Follow through with the left foot and step to the left side, quick (1 count).

5. Draw the right foot slowly to the arch of the left foot, weight remaining on the left foot, slow (2 counts).

TANGO PROMENADE

THE CRISSCROSS

The crisscross is a tango figure done sideways across the line of direction.

PRACTICE

As the man takes two steps to his left he pushes gently against the left side of the woman's torso with his right hand. As he pivots and steps to his right side he draws the woman sideways, maintaining the lead with his upper right arm. The shoulders *must* remain parallel while practicing the crisscross figure.

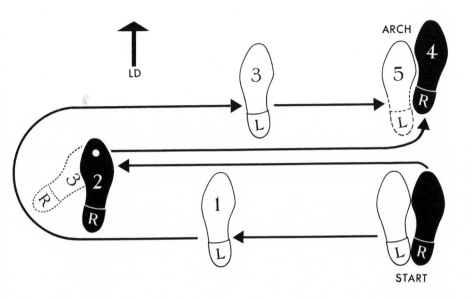

Man

1. Facing in the line of direction, in closed position, step to the side on the left foot, the right toe remaining in place, slow (2 counts).

2. Step across to the left side with the right foot, slow (2 counts).

3. Pivoting to the right on the right foot, step across with the left foot to the right side, quick (1 count).

4. Step to the side with the right foot, quick (1 count).

5. Draw the left foot slowly to the arch of the right foot, weight remaining on the right foot, slow (2 counts).

(Keep shoulders parallel at all times.)

TANGO—CRISSCROSS

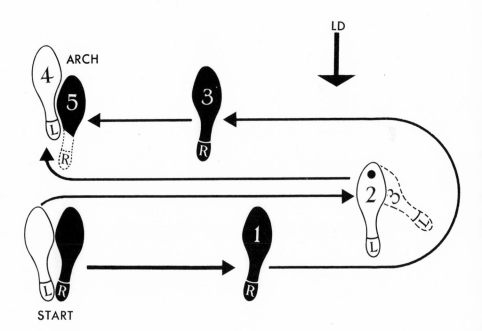

Woman

1. Backing in the line of direction, in closed position, step to the side on the right foot, the left toe remaining in place, slow (2 counts).

2. Step across to the right side with the left foot, slow (2 counts).

3. Pivoting to the left on the left foot, step across with the right foot to the left side, quick (1 count).

4. Step to the side with the left foot, quick (1 count).

5. Draw the right foot slowly to the arch of the left foot, weight remaining on the left foot, slow (2 counts).

(Keep shoulders parallel at all times.)

TANGO—CRISSCROSS

PUSH-AWAY BREAK

(TANGO)

Starting in closed position, partners take two slow steps and one quick step in the line of direction. On the quick step the man pushes the woman backward into open break position, releasing his right hand. Maintaining the open break position, partners step to the side on the second quick and arch on the slow.

The closed position may be resumed by taking two promenade steps sideways, closing on two quick steps, followed by an arch, the man placing his right hand under the woman's left shoulder blade.

1   2

THE RUN-AROUND

Here is an intriguing tango figure known as the run-around. Beginning with the man and woman both standing in promenade position, the man crosses his feet and pivots in place as the woman describes a circle around him, the figure ending in closed position.

3   4 and 5

Leading and following are an integral part of each other in this figure inasmuch as the man initiates and continues the woman's movement around him, which in turn causes him to pivot. The woman facilitates the movement by leaning slightly backward.

THE RUN-AROUND

Man

Stand in the line of direction in promenade position, feet together, the weight over the right foot.

1. Step sideways on the left foot, pushing the woman slightly to the left with the right hand, slow (2 counts).

2. Step across on the right foot to the left, continuing to push the woman to the left, slow (2 counts).

3.-4. Pivot on both feet, a half circle to the left, quick, quick (2 counts).

5. Bringing the girl into closed position, draw the left foot slowly to the arch of the right foot, weight remaining on the right foot, slow (2 counts).

Woman

Stand in the line of direction in promenade position, feet together, the weight over the left foot.

You are now going to describe a circle around the man, turning to the left.

1. Step forward on the right foot, turning slightly to the left, slow (2 counts).

2. Step forward on the left foot, continuing to turn left, slow (2 counts).

3. Step forward on the right foot, continuing to turn left, quick (1 count).

4. Step forward on the left foot, continuing to turn left, quick (1 count).

5. Pivoting on the left foot into closed position, draw the right foot slowly to the arch of the left foot, weight remaining on the left foot, slow (2 counts).

RUNNING STEP

Those who have mastered the preceding tango figures will find the running step a stimulating change. The running step is a variation in the basic tango rhythm—slow, slow, quick, quick, slow —in which a step is taken on the last slow instead of an arch (no weight).

The figure consists of walking in the line of direction to the slow, slow rhythm, running to the quick, quick, and walking to the slow. The man begins the figure with his left foot, the woman with the right foot. In repeating the figure, the man begins with the right foot, the woman with the left foot.

Starting in closed position, the figure may be done in the line of direction around the room, and in a smaller circle—partners tilting toward the center of the circle. In addition, the running step may be done as a side figure. Starting in closed position, facing sideways in the line of direction, partners step sideways in the basic rhythm, pivoting a half turn to the right on the last slow. With opposite sides facing in the line of direction, partners step sideways in the basic rhythm, pivoting another half turn to the right on the last slow.

It is important to *look* in the direction in which one is moving, keeping the shoulders *parallel*. On the first half of the figure the head and arms point in the direction in which one is moving. On the second half of the figure the head and elbows point in the direction in which one is moving.

THE SWIRL

For the tango enthusiast the swirl is the most glamorous figure of all. It has real audience appeal and when well executed "stops the show."

The figure consists of the man standing in place as he swirls the girl from side to side. In swirling, the woman describes a figure eight both in the floor pattern and through the body. In leading the swirl the man describes a figure eight in the torso. Since each swirl consists of half a turn, the man will have to lead the woman firmly with his right hand, while keeping the movement smooth and flowing.

The swirl may be done singly or several times in succession.

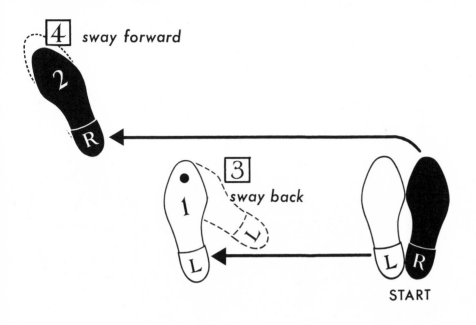

Man

1. Facing in the line of direction, in promenade position, step sideways on the left foot, slow (2 counts).

2. Step across on the right foot, slow (2 counts).

3. Turning the woman a half turn to her left, sway back in place on the left foot, slow (2 counts).

4. Turning the woman a half turn to her right, sway forward in place on the right foot, slow (2 counts).

(You have just completed a swirl. In order to complete a tango figure, we suggest adding two quick steps and a slow in closed position.)

TANGO—THE SWIRL

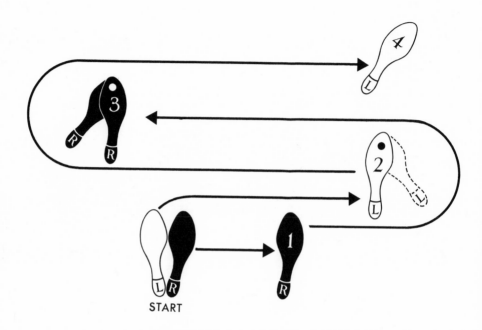

START

Woman

1. Facing in the line of direction, in promenade position, step sideways on the right foot, slow (2 counts).

2. Step across on the left, pivoting a half turn to the left while swinging the right leg across, slow (2 counts).

3. Step on the right foot, pivoting a half turn to the right, swinging the left leg across, slow (2 counts).

4. Step on the left foot, slow (2 counts).

(You have just completed a swirl. In order to complete a tango figure, we suggest pivoting on the left foot into closed position, followed by two quick steps and a slow).

TANGO—THE SWIRL

THE ROCK STEP (HABANERA)

However interesting the slow, slow, quick-quick, slow rhythm is in the tango, the dance would be incomplete without the so-called rock step (rocking the weight forward and back on the balls of the feet). The rock step rhythm is quick-quick, slow and requires one measure of music in 4/4 ♩ ♩ ♩ ♩time. Here is what it looks like:

QUICK   QUICK   SLOW

The rock step is based on the traditional Habanera rhythm in 4/4 time. Here it is:

This rhythm shows the influence of the Spanish, Negroid, and South American flavor that is so characteristic of the Latin-American dances.

PRACTICING THE ROCK STEP

The rock step may be done forward and backward and in a turn. It may be done in closed or step-out position. But before undertaking to practice these positions with a partner, it might be wise for you to learn the rock step alone. Here is a description of the step.

Man

1. Facing in the line of direction, step forward on the left foot, quick (1 count).

2. Stepping back on the ball of the right foot, rock back, quick (1 count).

3. Step forward on the left foot (the right foot follows through), slow (2 counts).

Repeat figure, starting forward on the right foot.

(Lead for the rock: Pull the woman slightly toward you on the second count, releasing the pressure of your right hand on the third count.)

Woman

1. Backing in the line of direction, step back on the ball of the right foot, quick (1 count).

2. Stepping forward on the left foot, rock forward, quick (1 count).

3. Step back on the ball of the right foot, allowing the weight to roll back on the whole foot (the left foot follows through), slow (2 counts).

Repeat figure, starting back on the ball of the left foot.

As a beginner you will find it easier to practice the rock step first in step-out position. After you have become familiar with the lead for the rock step in this position, you will find it quite easy to progress to the closed position. The transition of moving from one figure into the other can be done on the slow of the preceding figure.

TURNING

By using the basic step quick-quick, slow, a quarter turn in closed position may be done to the left or right.

For a more continuous turn, try stepping and rocking, using all quicks. For example, if the man is turning left, he steps forward on the left foot, quick, he steps back on the ball of the right foot, quick, three times in succession (6 counts), followed by a slow step, forward on the left foot (2 counts). The right foot is now released to begin the right turn. The figure may be repeated by stepping forward on the right foot and back on the ball of the left foot, three times in succession; followed by a slow step forward on the right foot as a transition to the left turn. Be sure to pivot as you turn either left or right.

In following the man for the left turn, the woman steps back on the ball of the right foot and forward on the left foot. To follow the man in turning right, the woman steps back on the ball of the left foot and steps forward on the right foot. (To become familiar with the entire figure, read the preceding description for the man.)

9. Charleston

THE Charleston is just as popular today as it was in the twenties when everyone was doing it. And even though the rhythm was tricky, nobody gave up! If you haven't done the Charleston while kicking up your heels to a Dixie Land band—here is your opportunity.

Start right off to learn the Charleston kicks. The twist step, which is so characteristic of the Charleston rhythm, will come gradually. And don't underestimate the time required for practice. The Charleston isn't as easy as you think. After you get going, try some combinations of your own. You'll probably stir up quite a breeze!

BASIC RHYTHM

The Music

The Charleston is done in 4/4 ♩ ♩ ♩ ♩ time. And the most characteristic thing about the rhythm is its jerky, staccato quality. Here is what the Charleston rhythm looks like:

As you can see the rhythm is highly syncopated. The shifting of the accent from the first beat to the eighth note, tied to the third beat, is what gives punch to the rhythm.

In practicing the steps to the music, however, you will find it easier to listen to the 4/4 ♩ ♩ ♩ ♩ time, which forms the background for the Charleston rhythm. And to make it even simpler, listen for an "and" before each beat. Here is what it looks like:

AND 1 AND 2 AND 3 AND 4

The "and" corresponds to the bending movement of the knee, which is taken before each movement or step. And it's the "and" rhythm that gives the Charleston its characteristic bounce!

The Dance

The Charleston is such a flexible dance it can be done as a solo, with a partner, or in a group (either in a straight line or in a circle), in which everybody has a chance to "get in the act." Therefore, the man and woman may use the same foot simultaneously since both will be facing forward. And while dancing the arms should be swung in opposition to the feet. For example, in stepping on the left foot, the arms swing across right. In stepping on the right foot, the arms swing across left.

We are going to start by learning the following steps: the point step and the kicks and progress to the twist step. Each figure will be fully described, the man and woman using the same directions.

PRACTICE

The Steps

You will find it easier to learn the point step first, progressing to the kicks. After you have mastered these steps, try the Charleston twist.

The Figures

Start right off by learning all the figures in place, in open position. Later you can progress to the promenade (moving forward or backward in the line of direction). After you have mastered the different steps you will find it fun to do them in closed position, the woman, as usual, stepping back on the opposite foot from the man.

The Charleston is done so informally that at any moment partners may break away, continuing to dance as they face each other. Whatever you do, have fun!

PRACTICING THE CHARLESTON

Man or Woman

I. *Step point:* in place (alternating right toe forward—left toe back).

Stand with feet together, the weight over the ball of the right foot.

    Bend right knee (count and).
1. Step forward on left foot (count 1).

    Bend left knee (count and).
2. Point right toe forward, straighten knees (count 2).

    Bend left knee (count and).
3. Step back on right foot (count 3).

    Bend right knee (count and).
4. Point left toe back, straighten knees (count 4).

Repeat, continuing to point the right toe forward, the left toe back.

II.   *Single kicks:* in place (alternating right and left leg).

Stand with feet together, the weight over the ball of the right foot.

      Bend right knee (count and).
1.   Step forward on left foot (count 1).

      Bend left knee (count and).
2.   Kick right leg forward, straighten knees (count 2).

      Bend left knee (count and).
3.   Step back on right foot (count 3).

      Bend right knee (count and).
4.   Kick left leg back, straighten knees (count 4).

Repeat, continuing to alternate right kick forward, left kick back.

III. *Double right kick:* in place.

Stand with feet together, the weight over the ball of the right foot.

　　Bend right knee (count and).
1.　Step forward on left foot (count 1).

　　Bend left knee (count and).
2.　Kick right leg forward, straighten knees (count 2).

　　Bend left knee (count and).
3.　Kick right leg back, straighten knees (count 3).

　　Bend left knee (count and).
4.　Step on right foot, bringing it to place, straighten knees (count 4).

　　Bend right knee (count and).

Double left kick: in place.

1.　Kick left leg forward, straighten knees (count 1).

　　Bend right knee (count and).
2.　Kick left leg back, straighten knees (count 2).

　　Bend right knee (count and).
3.　Step on left foot, bringing it to place, straighten knees (count 3).

The figure (the double right kick and double left kick) is now complete. To continue, repeat (and 4 and) of the double left kick, and continuing, by returning to the third count of the double right kick. The figure may now be repeated indefinitely.

　　Bend left knee (count and).
4.　Kick right leg forward (count 4).

　　Bend left knee (count and).

Promenade variation (double kicks):

To progress in the line of direction, step forward on the fourth count of the first half of figure number III (the right double kick) and on the third count of the second half of the figure (the left double kick). In other words, a forward step is taken after each double kick instead of bringing the foot back to place.

IV.   *Single diagonal kicks:* in place (alternating right and left leg).

Stand with feet together, the weight over the ball of the right foot.

    Bend right knee (count and).
1. Step sideward on left foot (count 1).

    Bend left knee (count and).
2. Kick right leg diagonally forward across left leg, straighten knees (count 2).

    Bend left knee (count and).
3. Step sideward on right foot, straighten knees (count 3).

    Bend right knee (count and).
4. Kick left leg diagonally across right leg, straighten knees (count 4).

Repeat, continuing to alternate the right and left leg.

V.   Double diagonal kicks: in place.

Right leg:

Stand with feet together, the weight over the ball of the right foot.

Bend right knee (count and).

1.   Step sideward on left foot (count 1).

Bend left knee (count and).

2.   Kick right leg diagonally forward across left leg, straighten knees (count 2).

Bend left knee (count and).

3.   Kick right leg back diagonally, straighten knees (count 3).

Bend left knee (count and).

4.   Step on right foot, bringing it to place, straighten knees (count 4).

Left leg:

Bend right knee (count and).

1.   Kick left leg diagonally forward across right leg, straighten knees (count 1).

Bend right knee (count and).

2.   Kick left leg back diagonally, straighten knees (count 2).

Bend right knee (count and).

3.   Step on left foot, bringing it to place, straighten knees (count 3).

The figure (the double diagonal right kick and double diagonal left kick) is now complete. To continue, repeat (and 4 and) of the double diagonal left kick, and continuing, by returning to the third count of the double diagonal right kick. The figure may now be repeated indefinitely.

Bend the left knee (count and).

4.   Kick right leg diagonally forward across left leg, straighten knees (count 4).

Bend the left knee (count and).

Promenade Variation (double diagonal kicks):

To progress in the line of direction, step forward on right foot on the fourth count of the first half of figure number V (the right double diagonal kicks) and on the third count of the second half of the figure (the left double diagonal kicks). In other words, a forward step is taken after each diagonal double kick instead of bringing the foot back to place.

THE CHARLESTON TWIST

The twist consists of pivoting in and out on the balls of the feet. Before undertaking to learn a figure, practice the twist in place. Read and practice the following section carefully:

Stand with the weight on both feet, heels touching, toes pointing out. Bending the knees, pivot in on the balls of the feet (count and), pivot out on the balls of the feet, straightening the knees, lower the heels (count 1). Repeat this exercise until the movement becomes automatic, remembering to bend, pivot— pivot, straighten.

Now you are ready to learn the twist figures.

I. *The twist:* in place (alternating left and right leg).

Standing in open position, heels together, toes pointing out, the weight on the right foot.

1. Bending the right knee, pivot in on the ball of the right foot, bringing the left leg up, knee turned in (count and), pivot out on the ball of the right foot, straightening knees, bring the left foot back to the heel of the right foot (toe pointed out), transferring the weight to the left foot (count 1).

2. Bending the left knee, pivot in on the ball of the left foot, bringing the right leg up, knee turned in (count and), pivot out on the ball of the left foot, straightening knees, bring the right foot back to the heel of the left foot (toe pointed out), transferring the weight to the right foot (count 2).

Repeat entire figure.

As a general rule, the foot is in the air when the toes point in, and a step is taken as the toes point out.

II. *The twist:* in place (stepping forward and back).

(This figure is really a variation of the point step in Figure I, except that one points forward and back with the ball of the foot.)

Standing in open position, heels together, toes pointing out, the weight on the right foot.

1. Bending the right knee, pivot in on the ball of the right foot, bringing the left leg up, knee turned in (count and), pivot out on the ball of the right foot, straightening knees, bring the left leg down, stepping forward on the left foot, transferring the weight (count 1).

2. Bending the left knee, pivot in on the ball of the left foot, bringing the right leg up, knee turned in (count and), pivot out on the ball of the left foot, straightening knees, bring the right leg down, the ball of the right foot touching the floor —no weight (count 2).

3. Bending the left knee, pivot in on the ball of the left foot, bringing the right leg up, knee turned in (count and), pivot out on the ball of the left foot, straightening knees, bring the right leg down, stepping back on the right foot, transferring the weight (count 3).

4. Bending the right knee, pivot in on the ball of the right foot, bringing the left leg up, knee turned in (count and), pivot out on the ball of the right foot, straightening knees, bring the left leg down, the ball of the left foot touching the floor —no weight (count 4).

You have now stepped forward on the left foot, pointing with the ball of the right foot, followed by stepping back on the right foot and pointing with the ball of the left foot. To continue, repeat the entire figure, pointing forward and back.

10. One-Step

The one-step is a fast, snappy affair in which every beat in a 4/4 measure is accented. As the name of the dance implies, one step is taken to every beat in the music. The dance has as much zip as a good, peppy march and is just as much fun to keep time to.

For those who like the spectacular, the one step continues to be tops.

PRACTICING THE ONE-STEP

Now that you have learned the medium-slow foxtrot, you are ready to tackle a one-step. And although the one-step can be done in closed, promenade, or step-out position, we are going to start off with variations of these figures—the closed position with a right turn, the promenade with a pivot turn, and throw-over from side to side. Each figure is fully described.

Start off by learning the closed position and progress to the right turn in the closed position. For variety, you might insert the turn-under at the end of either of these figures. Remember, there is nothing set about the progression of one figure to another—so have fun making up your own combinations.

After you have mastered the preceding figures try the throw-over. To get into the open position from which you begin the throw-over figure, start from a closed position and throw the woman to your right side. You are now both facing in the line of direction. The transition from a throw-over to a closed position is made by the man stepping in front of the woman. He is now backing in the line of direction. To progress forward again in the line of direction, a pivot turn may be inserted. Incidentally, it is not necessary to keep repeating the throw-over from side to side as shown in the diagram. Occasionally, a half throw-over figure may be done, for example, tossing the woman from the starting position to the opposite side and continuing in the line of direction.

At this point you are ready to tackle the pivot turn in place. Once you get going, you will find yourself progressing around the room in high speed. And for a real challenge, try the Peabody turn. It represents the pinnacle for every good dancer. So *do* try it.

After practicing these figures you will find yourself moving from one position to another with the greatest of ease—the one-step being the simplest of all dances.

At all times, stay on the balls of the feet.

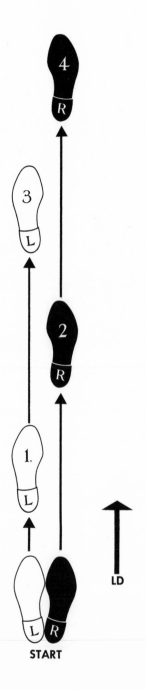

4. Step forward on the right foot, quick (1 count).

3. Step forward on the left foot, quick (1 count).

2. Step forward on the right foot, quick (1 count).

1. Step forward on the left foot, quick (1 count).

Man

ONE-STEP—CLOSED POSITION

Woman

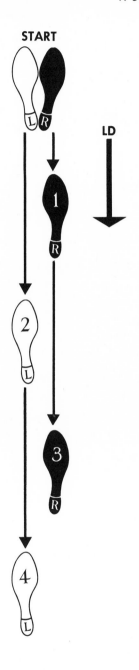

1. Step back on the right foot, quick (1 count).

2. Step back on the left foot, quick (1 count).

3. Step back on the right foot, quick (1 count).

4. Step back on the left foot, quick (1 count).

ONE-STEP CLOSED POSITION

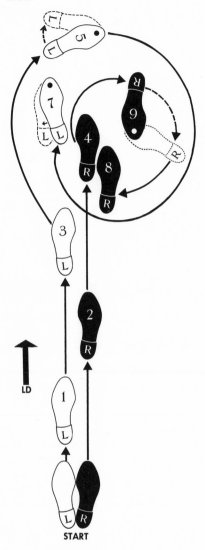

8. Step back on the right foot in the line of direction, quick (1 count).

7. Step on the left foot, continuing to the right, pivoting slightly, quick (1 count). You are now facing in the line of direction.

6. Step on the right foot, continuing to the right, pivoting slightly, quick (1 count).

5. Step on the left foot to the right, pivoting slightly, quick (1 count).

1-4. Walk forward left, right left, right, quick (4 counts).

(The three pivot steps describe a complete turn to the right, the dotted feet indicating the direction of the pivot turn).

Turn the book in your hand to correspond with the direction in which you are turning.

Man

RIGHT TURN
ONE-STEP—CLOSED POSITION

Woman

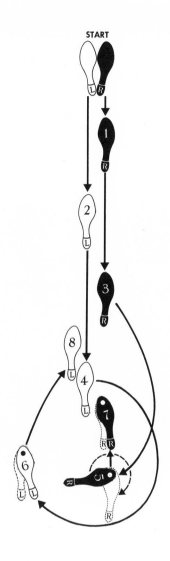

(The three pivot steps describe a complete turn to the right, the dotted feet indicating the direction of the pivot turn).

1-4. Walk backward right, left, right, left, quicks (4 counts).

5. Step back on the right foot, turning to the right, pivoting slightly, quick (1 count).

6. Step back on the left foot, turning to the right, pivoting slightly, quick (1 count).

7. Step back on the right foot, continuing to the right, pivoting slightly, quick (1 count). You are now backing in the line of direction.

8. Step forward on the left foot, quick (1 count).

Turn the book in your hand to correspond with the direction in which you are turning.

RIGHT TURN
ONE-STEP—CLOSED POSITION

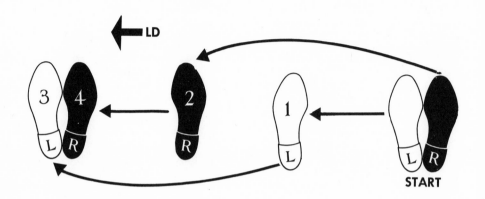

Man

1. Step sideways on left foot, quick (1 count).

2. Step across in front of the left foot with right foot, quick (1 count), with hands clasped, raise the woman's right arm to prepare for the right turn.

3. Step sideways on left foot, quick (1 count), turning the woman under her right arm and releasing your right hand.

4. Close right foot against left foot, transferring weight, quick (1 count), while bringing the right hand back to the left side of the woman's torso as she completes the turn; lower arms to shoulder level.

THE TURN-UNDER
(PROMENADE)
ONE-STEP

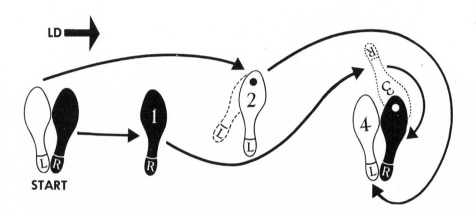

Woman

1.   Step sideways on right foot, quick (1 count).

2.   Step across in front of the right foot with left foot, pivoting slightly to the right, quick (1 count), raising the right arm to prepare for the right turn.

3.   Step sideways, pivoting (turning) on the ball of right foot (left foot follows through), making a complete right turn, quick (1 count), right fingers turning in man's left hand, while releasing left hand from man's right shoulder (keeping hands vertical while turning).

4.   Close left foot against right foot, transferring weight, quick (1 count), drop left hand to man's right shoulder; lower arms to shoulder level.

THE TURN-UNDER
(PROMENADE)
ONE-STEP

ONE-STEP—OPEN POSITION
THROW-OVER—SIDE TO SIDE

The throw-over figure is almost a continuous motion in which the initial lead for throwing the woman to the opposite side occurs on the second beat, the follow-through of the arm swinging the women over on the third beat.

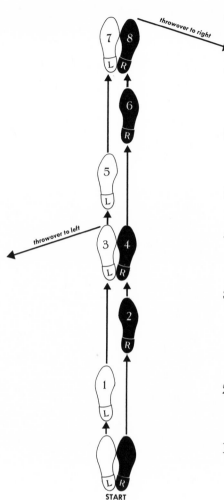

8. Step forward on the right foot, closing right foot against the left foot, quick (1 count).

7. Step forward on left foot, catching the woman with your right hand, quick (1 count).

6. Step forward on the right foot, throwing the woman over to your right side, quick (1 count).

5. Step forward on left foot, quick (1 count).

4. Step forward on the right foot, closing right foot against left foot, quick (1 count).

3. Step forward on left foot, catching the woman with your left hand, quick (1 count). The left hand is now under the woman's right shoulder blade.

2. Step forward on the right foot, throwing the woman over to your left side, quick (1 count).

1. Standing in open position, with the woman on your right side, the right hand under her left shoulder blade, the left arm at your side, step forward on the left foot, quick (1 count).

Man

THROW-OVER—SIDE TO SIDE
ONE-STEP—OPEN POSITION

8. Close left foot against the right foot, transferring weight, quick (1 count).

7. Step sideways on the right foot, pivoting (turning) on the ball of the right foot (left foot follows through), making a complete right turn, quick (1 count), dropping your left hand on the man's right shoulder.

6. Step forward on left foot, pivoting slightly to the right to prepare for throw-over to right side, quick (1 count).

5. Step forward on right foot, quick (1 count).

4. Close left foot against right foot, transferring weight, quick (1 count).

3. Step across in front of left foot to left side, pivoting (turning) on the ball of the right foot (left foot follows through), making a complete left turn, quick (1 count), dropping your right hand on the man's left shoulder.

2. Step forward on left foot, pivoting slightly to the left to prepare for throw-over to left side, quick (1 count).

1. Standing in open position, on the man's right side, left hand on his right shoulder, the right arm at your side, step forward on the right foot, quick (1 count).

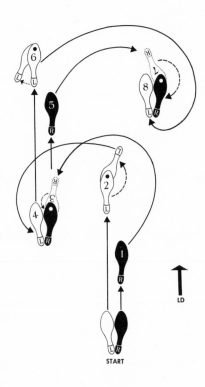

Turn the book in your hand to correspond with the direction in which you are turning.

Woman

THROW-OVER—SIDE TO SIDE
ONE-STEP—OPEN POSITION

THE PROMENADE PIVOT TURN

The promenade pivot turn consists of walking in the line of direction in promenade position, turning into closed position, and opening out to continue the figure.

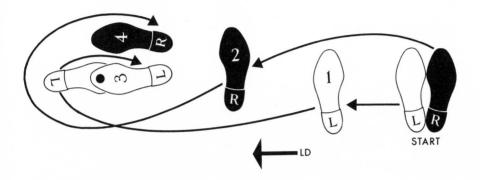

Turn the book in your hand to correspond with the direction in which you are turning.

NOTE: It is important to grasp the woman firmly with the right hand on the third beat as you pivot into closed position. It is equally important to release the pressure of the right hand on the fourth beat as you open into promenade position.

4.   Continuing to pivot right, step on right foot, quick (1 count).

3.   Stepping back in the line of direction on the left foot, pivot to the right into closed position, quick (1 count).

2.   Step across in front of the left foot, with right foot, quick (1 count).

1.   Step sideways on the left foot, quick (1 count).

Facing in the line of direction in promenade position, weight over the right foot.

Man

PROMENADE PIVOT TURN
ONE-STEP

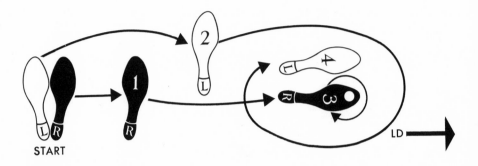

Turn the book in your hand to correspond with the direction in which you are turning.

Woman

Facing in the line of direction in promenade position, weight over the left foot.

1. Step sideways on the right foot, quick (1 count).

2. Step across in front of the right foot with left foot, quick (1 count).

3. Stepping forward in the line of direction on the right foot, pivot to the right into closed position, quick (1 count).

4. Continuing to pivot right, step on left foot, quick (1 count).

NOTE: A firm pressure of the left hand should be exerted on the man's right shoulder as you pivot into closed position on the third beat, while placing your right foot between the man's feet on the pivot turn. And remember to release the pressure of the left hand on the fourth beat as you open into promenade position.

PROMENADE PIVOT TURN
ONE-STEP

THE PIVOT TURN

The pivot turn we are describing consists of turning in place in closed position. Before practicing the pivot turn in place special attention should be given to the position of the feet. Therefore, the following description should be read carefully.

On the first count of the pivot turn the man steps back on his left foot, turning slightly to the right, as the woman steps forward on her right foot. This results in the *inside* of the man's right foot touching the *inside* of the woman's right foot. On the second count the man actually begins the pivot. It is important to maintain the clamped position of the feet as the pivot continues.

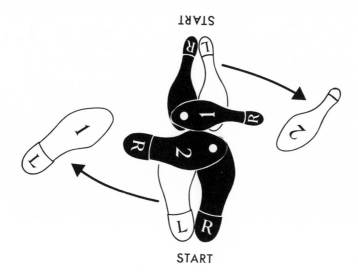

START

As soon as you have mastered the turn in place you will find it even more fun to progress around the room while turning. In order to progress in the line of direction it will be necessary to push off forcibly from one foot to the other, keeping the feet clamped while pivoting on the balls of both feet. To maintain one's balance while turning continuously, the man should hold the woman firmly with his right hand, the woman arching her back while pressing her left hand against the man's right shoulder.

Remember, it is a difficult turn to execute and, therefore, requires plenty of practice.

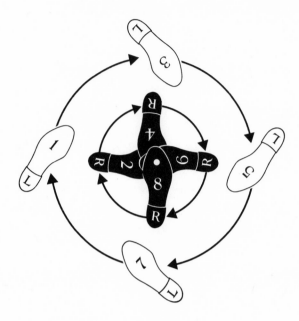

Turn the book in your hand to correspond with the direction in which you are turning.

Man

Stand with feet together, the weight over the right foot.

1. Turning slightly to the right, step back on the left foot, quick (1 count).

2. Step forward on the right foot, pivoting to the right, quick (1 count).

3. Step back on the left foot, quick (1 count).

4. Step forward on the right foot, pivoting to the right, quick (1 count).

(You have now done a half turn to the right. To complete the turn follow the diagram [5 through 8].)

PIVOT TURN
ONE-STEP—CLOSED POSITION

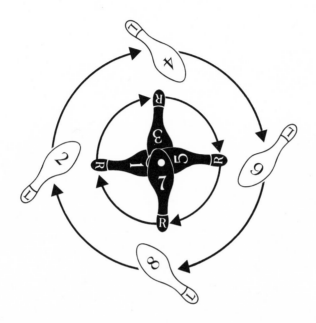

Turn the book in your hand to correspond with the direction in which you are turning.

Woman

Stand with feet together, the weight over the left foot.

1. Step forward on the right foot, pivoting slightly to the right, quick (1 count).

2. Step back on the left foot, quick (1 count).

3. Step forward on the right foot, pivoting to the right, quick (1 count).

4. Step back on the left foot, quick (1 count).

(You have now done a half turn to the right. To complete the turn follow the diagram [5 through 8].)

PIVOT TURN
ONE-STEP—CLOSED POSITION

1 and **2**   **3**

PEABODY TURN

The Peabody turn is one of the most fascinating figures in the one-step. It consists of moving in line of direction in right step-out position, turning in closed position, and crossing into left step-out position. The figure is tricky to execute and, therefore, requires careful study.

PRACTICING THE PEABODY TURN

Because of the speed at which the Peabody turn is executed, it will be necessary for the man to *increase* the pressure of his lead

4   5 and 6

as he pivots into closed position on the third count. The pressure is released as he finishes the pivot on the fourth count. A smooth, continuous movement will have to be maintained while making the transitions from one step-out position to the other. Therefore, all leads will have to be given promptly and quickly.

The Peabody figure we are describing ends in left step-out position on the sixth count. In order to repeat the figure the sixth count becomes the transition from left step-out position to right step-out position. Therefore, it will be necessary for the man to move the woman *sharply* to her left on the sixth count into right step-out position. From here on the figure may be continued.

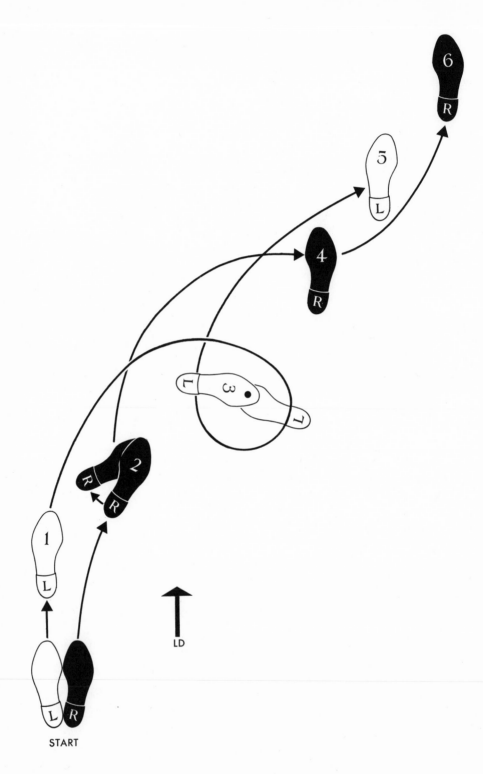

START

LD

Turn the book in your hand to correspond with the direction in which you are turning.

6. Step forward on the right foot, quick (1 count).

5. Step on the left foot, diagonally forward into left step-out position, quick (1 count).

4. Continuing to pivot right on the left foot, step on the right foot, completing the turn, quick (1 count).
(You are now facing in the line of direction.)

3. Step forward on the left foot, pivoting to the right into closed position, quick (1 count).
(Your back is now in the line of direction.)

2. Step forward on the right foot, turning slightly to the right, quick (1 count).

1. Step forward on the left foot, quick (1 count).

Facing in the line of direction in step-out position (right side to right side).

Man

ONE-STEP—PEABODY TURN

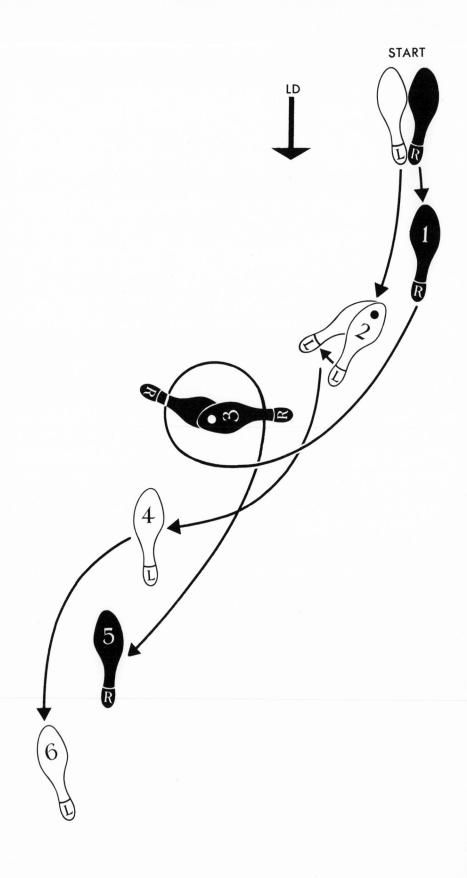

Turn the book in your hand to correspond with the direction in which you are turning.

Woman

Backing in the line of direction in step-out position (right side to right side).

1. Step backward on the right foot, quick (1 count).

2. Step backward on the left foot, turning slightly to the right, quick (1 count).

3. Step backward on the right foot, pivoting in closed position, quick (1 count).
   (You are now facing in the line of direction.)

4. Continuing to pivot right on the right foot, step on the left foot, completing the turn, quick (1 count).
   (Your back is now in the line of direction).

5. Step on the right foot, diagonally back into left step-out position, quick (1 count).

6. Step backward on the left foot, quick (1 count).

ONE-STEP—PEABODY TURN

THE PASO DOBLE

The *paso doble* is a one-step done to Spanish music in march time. The melodies and rhythms have a bright, spicy quality that is so characteristically Spanish.

Any of the preceding one-step figures may be used while dancing the *paso doble*. The customary walking step, however, done in the line of direction, may be varied occasionally by partners moving sideways—stepping and closing.

Anyone who has mastered the one-step in the American fox-trot will find the rhythms of the *paso doble* irresistible. So try a *paso doble*—next time one is played.

11. Merengue

OF ALL the Latin-American dances to arrive here from the Caribbean, the merengue is, by far, the easiest to execute. Although there are several varieties of the dance, the Dominican merengue is probably the most popular. The dance may be done in a light, breezy manner or in a suave, sophisticated style. But whichever mood you prefer, you will find it easy to learn the Dominican merengue.

THE BASIC RHYTHM

The music of the merengue is in 2/4 ♩ ♩ time. The basic rhythm requires two measures of music, the accent occurring on the first beat. In counting the steps to the music, however, we are going to use a 4/4 ♩ ♩ ♩ ♩ rhythm. Here it is:

THE BASIC STEP

The basic step of the merengue is done in 4/4 ♩ ♩ ♩ ♩ time. The basic rhythm is quick, quick, quick, quick. Here it is:

In dancing the merengue, a step-close is taken to the side and repeated—the accents occurring on the first and third beats.

STEP   CLOSE   STEP   CLOSE

In practicing the basic step of the merengue, a slight dip is taken on the side step. And it is this dipping movement of the knee—whether a step is taken sideward, forward, or backward—that gives the merengue its characteristic style.

We are going to learn the sideward basic step, the left turn, the right turn, and the forward and back basic step. Each of these figures is described. Some mention will be made regarding the forward and back left turn, the forward and back rock, and the merengue twist. Later we will describe the merengue walk and include numerous variations of the walk.

Now, we will proceed to learn the basic step.

MERENGUE
SIDEWARD BASIC STEP

Man

Stand in closed position, feet together, the weight over the right foot.

1. Stepping to the left side on the left foot, dip the knee, quick (1 count).

2. Drawing the right foot to the left foot, transfer the weight, quick (1 count).

3. Stepping to the left side on the left foot, dip the knee, quick (1 count).

4. Drawing the right foot to the left foot, transfer the weight, quick (1 count).

The entire figure may now be repeated to the right by arching (no weight) the right foot to the left foot on the fourth count.

MERENGUE
SIDEWARD BASIC STEP

Woman

Stand in closed position, feet together, the weight over the left foot.

1. Stepping to the right side on the right foot, dip the knee, quick (1 count).

2. Drawing the left foot to the right foot, transfer the weight, quick (1 count).

3. Stepping to the right side on the right foot, dip the knee, quick (1 count).

4. Drawing the left foot to the right foot, transfer the weight, quick (1 count).

The entire figure may now be repeated to the left by arching (no weight) the left foot to the right foot on the fourth count.

MERENGUE
LEFT TURN

Man

Stand in closed position, feet together, the weight over the right foot.

1. Pivoting on the right foot to the left, step across on the left foot, dipping, quick (1 count).

2. Continuing to the left, step to the side with the right foot, quick (1 count).

3. Continuing to the left, pivoting on the right foot, step across on the left foot, dipping, quick (1 count).

4. Continuing to the left, step to the side with the right foot, quick (1 count).

MERENGUE
LEFT TURN

Woman

Stand in closed position, feet together, the weight over the left foot.

1. Turning to the left, step to the side on the right foot, dipping, quick (1 count).

2. Continuing to the left, pivoting on the right foot, step across on the left foot, quick (1 count).

3. Continuing to the left, step to the side on the right foot, dipping, quick (1 count).

4. Continuing to the left, pivoting on the right foot, step across on the left foot, quick (1 count).

MERENGUE
RIGHT TURN

Man

Stand in closed position, feet together, the weight over the right foot.

1. Turning to the right, step to the side on the left foot, dipping, quick (1 count).

2. Continuing to the right, pivoting on the left foot, step across on the right foot, quick (1 count).

3. Continuing to the right, step to the side on the left foot, dipping, quick (1 count).

4. Continuing to the right, pivoting on the left foot, step across on the right foot, quick (1 count).

MERENGUE
RIGHT TURN

Woman

Stand in closed position, feet together, the weight over the left foot.

1. Pivoting on the left foot to the right, step across on the right foot, dipping, quick (1 count).

2. Continuing to turn right, step to the side on the left foot, quick (1 count).

3. Continuing to turn right, pivoting on the left foot, step across on the right foot, dipping, quick (1 count).

4. Continuing to turn right, step to the side on the left foot, quick (1 count).

MERENGUE—FORWARD AND BACK
BASIC STEP

Man or Woman

Stand with feet together, the weight over the right foot.

1. Step forward on the left foot, dipping, quick (1 count).

2. Close the right foot to the left foot, transferring the weight, quick (1 count).

3. Step back on the left foot, dipping, quick (1 count).

4. Close the right foot to the left, transferring the weight, quick (1 count).

PRACTICE (VARIATIONS)

In dancing the forward and back step with a partner in closed position, the woman, as usual, starts with her right foot. The forward and back step may also be done turning to the left. From here, you may progress to the forward and back rock, which con-

sists of the man rocking forward and back on the left foot, while
pivoting on the right foot. (The woman uses the opposite foot.)
In practicing the rock the body swings freely from side to side.

Having mastered the preceding figures, you will enjoy the
challenge of the merengue twist. Here is the figure: With partners
starting in closed position, the man does the basic step in place
while twisting the woman from side to side. As the man twists
the woman to her right, she pivots and dips on her left foot, closing
with her right foot. As he twists her to her left, she pivots and dips
on her left foot, closing with her right foot. It is important for the
woman to keep her feet together as she twists from side to side.

MERENGUE WALK

However intriguing the dip-step may be in the merengue, there is a secondary rhythm, known as the merengue walk, that is also attractive. It is easy to do and gives variety to the dance.

The merengue walk consists of placing the foot (no weight), knee bent, the weight following as the step is taken. (For a complete analysis of the step, see pages 66 and 67—the rumba movement.) The merengue walk can be done to the side, forward, or back, and in a circle—in closed or outside position.

In addition to the preceding figures, the merengue walk can be done quite freely in open breaks. At any moment, partners may break away, continuing in the merengue walk. The most characteristic break, however, is done from side to side. Starting in closed position, the woman's right hand in the man's left hand, the man marks time in place while transferring the woman to his left side, followed by transferring the woman to his right side, taking the woman's left hand in his right hand. In moving from side to side, the woman takes four walking steps in a half circle in front of her partner, bowing slightly to him on the fourth step.

And finally, for something tricky, the merengue walk can be done, moving to the left side, with the woman's back against the man's right shoulder, partners facing forward. The man clasps the woman's waist with his right hand, holding her left hand in his left hand.

And now that you have become a merengue enthusiast, try some variations of your own.

12. Lindy

FOR those who like plenty of action—the lindy continues to hold its own. The dance is of Negroid origin and has a folksy quality that offers numerous opportunities for variety in the way of "breaks" and steps. The so-called solid beat in the music gives the dance its characteristic lilt and bounce. But remember, a lindy doesn't have to be hot or fast to be good. A medium tempo will give ample opportunity for letting go while still keeping things under control.

And don't get discouraged while learning the lindy if you find the going rough. Although it is an exciting dance, it is the most difficult to co-ordinate. So take it easy.

THE BASIC RHYTHM

The lindy is in 4/4 ♩ ♩ ♩ ♩ time. The basic rhythm is slow, slow, quick-quick. Two half notes ♩ ♩ followed by two quarter notes ♩ ♩ give us ♩ ♩ ♩ ♩ (six counts). As you will see this rhythm results in an overlapping within a 4/4 measure. Here is what it looks like:

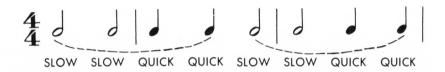

SLOW   SLOW   QUICK   QUICK   SLOW   SLOW   QUICK   QUICK

In dancing the lindy, a "dig" (pushing the ball of the foot into the floor, followed by bringing the heel down, transferring the weight from the supporting foot) is done to a slow, and repeated, followed by two quick steps (six counts). Here is the rhythm:

DIG — STEP   DIG — STEP   STEP   STEP   DIG — STEP   DIG — STEP   STEP   STEP

The breaks are also done to the slow, slow, quick-quick rhythm. (A break is a figure done close to or away from one's partner.) And although the steps and breaks are an integral part of each other, we are going to start with the footwork and progress to the breaks.

THE BASIC STEP

Before taking up the basic step (slow, slow, quick-quick), we are going to practice the rhythm that underlies the dig steps. The following paragraphs should be read and practiced carefully.

Man or woman, stand with the feet together, the weight over the ball of the right foot. Dig with the ball of the left foot, bending the knee (count 1), bring the left heel down, transferring the weight from the right foot to the left foot, straightening the left knee (count 2). You have now done one slow.

Dig with the ball of the right foot, bending the knee (count 3), bring the right heel down, transferring the weight from the left foot to the right foot, straightening the right knee (count 4). You have now done two slows to the count of 1–2, 3–4.

Practice the dig steps in place to the 1–2, 3–4 count. As soon as you have become familiar with this rhythm, practice the dig steps to slows, omitting the 1–2, 3–4 count. Practice until the rhythm becomes automatic and keep a light, bouncy knee motion, which is one of the more characteristic things about the lindy. We are now ready to proceed to the quick-quick rhythm.

The quick steps are taken by bringing the ball of the foot in contact with the floor first, allowing the weight to roll onto the whole foot. Two steps are taken in succession (quick-quick). The knees should be relaxed so that the change of weight in stepping can be done quickly.

Now, practice the entire basic step in place, dig step, dig step, step, step (slow, slow, quick-quick).

You are now ready to tackle the breaks.

BREAKS

The following breaks, with the accompanying footwork, will be described in detail: the push-away, the turn-under, the elbow break, and the Texas Tommy. Later we will describe variations of these breaks after you have mastered the lindy in place.

The push-away break will be described simultaneously for the man and woman since both are doing the same figure. The steps, however, may be practiced alone, the man, as usual, beginning on the left foot, the woman beginning on the right foot. All other breaks will be described separately for the man and woman.

There are various ways of doing breaks. They may be done

forward, sideward, backward, and while turning. And since the lindy is done so freely, the breaks may be done close to or away from one's partner.

In learning the breaks start off with the push-away, progressing to the turn-under and on to the elbow break. For something really fancy, try the Texas Tommy. And be sure to master one break at a time.

LEADING OR FOLLOWING

After warming up (doing the dig step in place), the man begins to throw the woman out on the first break. After she is thrown out, the man pulls the woman in. (This throwing out and pulling in is the most characteristic thing about the lindy.) Both the man and the woman's knees should be bent on the pull in, the woman leaning out, keeping her arm firm but not rigid.

The elbows should be kept close to the body in a free, swinging movement. And since the right or left hand is used freely in starting breaks, the leads should be given promptly and quickly. (Remember, the lindy really moves!)

And finally, while holding the woman's right hand in the usual lindy clasp, the man's left hand should be sufficiently relaxed so that the woman's fingers can pivot while making the transitions on the breaks.

PUSH-AWAY BREAK

Man and Woman

(The push-away break consists of the man pushing the woman out to the right, both stepping back diagonally on the outside foot.)

Facing in the line of direction, in promenade position, the man's right hand under the woman's left shoulder blade, the woman's left hand on the man's right shoulder, the hands joined in the lindy clasp, stand with feet together, the weight over the ball of the inside foot.

1. Dig with the outside foot, bring heel down, transferring the weight from the inside foot, slow (2 counts).

2. Dig with the inside foot, bring heel down, transferring the weight from the outside foot, slow (2 counts).

3. Pushing the woman away with the lindy hand clasp, opening out slightly, both step back diagonally on the outside foot, the ball of the inside foot remaining in place (no weight), quick (1 count).

4. Pulling the woman in, both step forward on the inside foot, closing with the outside foot, quick (1 count).

You are now in the original promenade position.

THE TURN-UNDER

Man

(This figure consists of turning the woman right and then left under her right arm.)

Facing in the line of direction, in promenade position, the woman on your right side, feet together, the weight over the ball of the right foot.

Right turn:

1. Dig with the left foot, bring the heel down, transferring the weight from the right foot while raising the woman's right arm to prepare for the turn-under, slow (2 counts).

2. With hands still raised in the lindy clasp, turn the woman with your right hand under her right arm, digging with the right foot, slow (2 counts).

3. Step back on the left foot, quick (1 count).

4. Step forward on the right foot, quick (1 count).

(With the hands still raised in the lindy clasp, you are now facing your partner.)

Left turn:

1. Dig with the left foot, bring the heel down, transferring the weight from the right foot while turning the woman to the left with your left hand, slow (2 counts).

2. Continuing to turn the woman left, dig with the right foot, transferring the weight from the left foot, slow (2 counts).

3. Step forward on the left foot, quick (1 count).

4. Step on the right foot, quick (1 count).

You are now back in the original promenade position with the right hand under the woman's left shoulder blade, the left hand lowered in the lindy clasp.

THE TURN-UNDER

Woman

(This figure consists of a right and then a left turn done under your right arm.)

Facing in the line of direction, in promenade position, the man on your left side, feet together, weight over the ball of the left foot.

Right turn:

1. Dig with the right foot, bring the heel down, transferring the weight from the left foot while raising the right arm to prepare for the turn-under, slow (2 counts).

2. Turning under your right arm, fingers turning in the man's left hand, dig with the left foot, pivoting right on the ball of the left foot, the right foot follows through, slow (2 counts). You are now backing in the line of direction.

3. Step back on the right foot, quick (1 count).

4. Step back on the left foot, quick (1 count).

(With the hands still raised in the lindy clasp, you are now facing your partner.)

Left turn:

1. Dig with the right foot, bring the heel down, transferring the weight from the left foot, slow (2 counts).

2. Turning left under your right arm, dig with the left foot, pivoting left on the ball of the left foot, the right foot follows through, slow (2 counts).

3. Continuing to turn left, step on the right foot, quick (1 count).

4. Step forward on the left foot, quick (1 count).

You are now back in your original promenade position with the left hand placed on the man's right shoulder blade, the right hand lowered in the lindy clasp.

THE ELBOW BREAK

Man

(The elbow break is done by snapping the woman in quickly toward your left side with the left hand, turning her quickly to the right with the right hand, and catching her right hand on the recovery of her turn, snapping her about with a left turn. In other words, the woman pivots quickly to the right, followed by a quick pivot turn to the left.)

Facing in the line of direction, in promenade position.

1. Dig with the left foot; pulling the woman toward you, bring the heel down, transferring the weight from the right foot, slow (2 counts).

2. Turning the woman quickly into a right pivot turn, dig with the right foot, transferring the weight from the left foot, slow (2 counts).

3. Catching the woman on the recovery of her right turn, swing her around to the left, stepping on the left foot, quick (1 count).

4. Step on the right foot, quick (1 count).

You are now in your original promenade position, the right hand under the woman's left shoulder blade, the left hand joined in a lindy clasp.

THE ELBOW BREAK

Woman

(The elbow break consists of pivoting quickly to the right followed by a complete pivot turn to the left.)

Facing in the line of direction, in promenade position.

1. Dig forward with the right foot, turning slightly to the left, bring the heel down, transferring the weight from the left foot, slow (2 counts).

2. Turning to the right, dig with the left foot, pivoting on the left foot, transferring the weight from the right foot, slow (2 counts). You have now done a complete right turn.

3. Step across in front of the left foot, with the right foot, pivoting quickly to the left on the ball of the right foot, quick (1 count).

4. Continuing to turn left, step on the left foot, quick (1 count).

You are now back in your original promenade position, the left hand on the man's right shoulder, your right hand joined in the lindy clasp.

THE TEXAS TOMMY

Man

(The Texas Tommy consists of snapping the woman into a right pivot turn, while backing up. With your right hand clasped in the woman's right hand, which is behind her back, the woman is snapped out into a right pivot turn.)

Facing in the line of direction, in promenade position.

1. Dig with the left foot; clasping the woman's right hand behind her back, bring the heel down, transferring the weight from the right foot, slow (2 counts).

2. Snap the woman into a right turn, digging with the right foot; bring the heel down, transferring the weight from the left foot, slow (2 counts).

3. Step back on the left foot, pulling the woman into the right turn, quick (1 count).

4. Continuing to pull the woman, step back on the right foot, quick (1 count).

You are now facing your partner in an open break. To resume the original promenade position, take two digs forward (2 slows), pulling the woman toward you; and take two steps in place (2 quicks), putting your right hand under the woman's left shoulder blade.

THE TEXAS TOMMY

Woman

(The Texas Tommy consists of a right pivot turn while traveling away from the man. Your right hand, which is across behind your back, is clasped in the man's right hand, as he snaps you into the right turn.)

Facing in the line of direction, in promenade position.

1. Dig with the right foot; pivoting slightly to the right, while clasping the man's right hand behind your back, bring the heel down, transferring the weight from the left foot, slow (2 counts).

2. Continuing to the right, dig with the left foot, pivoting on the ball of the left foot, transferring the weight from the right foot, slow (2 counts).

3. Still continuing to unwind in the right hand clasp, step back on the right foot, quick (1 count).

4. Step back on the left foot, quick (1 count).

You are now facing your partner in an open break. To resume the original promenade position, take two digs forward (2 slows), and two steps in place (2 quicks), dropping your left hand back to the man's right shoulder blade.

VARIATIONS

Now that you have learned the breaks in place, you can begin to add variety by pivoting and traveling. (Traveling in the lindy means moving from one place to another and it can be done quite freely.) It would be pretty dull if the man had to stay in one place while the woman moves about. (And after all, there is no reason why the woman should steal the whole show.)

Traveling or pivoting is usually done on the quick-quicks, the man or woman backing away or around each other. And since one can do as one pleases in the lindy, there are no transitions to worry about! Once the lead and follow-through are indicated, one can really let go.

THE DOUBLE LINDY STEP

Those who are really good may want to dress up the lindy step that has been described by doing a double lindy.

Here is what the double lindy step looks like:

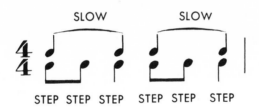

Three quick steps are taken in time to the usual slow (dig step). The double lindy step can be done in any of the open breaks. It will add variety to your lindy, and at least it's worth a try!

13. Viennese Waltz

NOW that you have learned the American waltz, try something a little more giddy. The Viennese waltz with its lilt and speed is fun to do, and the melodies are delightful.

For a grand occasion—like a formal dance for instance—there is nothing like a Viennese waltz. It adds sparkle and gaiety and is worth that extra effort required to learn the pivot turn.

PRACTICING THE VIENNESE WALTZ

The most characteristic thing about a Viennese waltz is its speed and the so-called pivot turn. (A pivot, as you know, consists of turning on the ball of the foot.)

It will be wise, therefore, for you to practice the forward and backward turns slowly. After you have mastered your own part, begin to practice with a partner.

Be sure to lean away slightly from your partner as you turn. It will help both of you to maintain your balance. The man should hold his right hand under the woman's left shoulder blade firmly, while turning, and the woman should maintain a firm hold on the back of the man's right shoulder blade.

The basic figure of the Viennese waltz is really quite simple, so you should have no difficulty in mastering this dance.

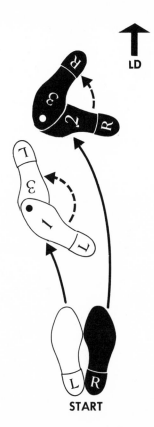

START

You are now backing in the line of direction.

3. Pivot on the balls of both feet, making another quarter turn to the left, transferring the weight to the left foot as the left heel touches the toe of the right foot (1 count).

2. Follow through with the right foot and take a short step to the right side (1 count).

1. Chest leading, step forward on left foot, making a quarter turn to the left (1 count).

Facing in the line of direction, feet together, the weight over the ball of the right foot.

Man

FORWARD HALF TURN
VIENNESE WALTZ

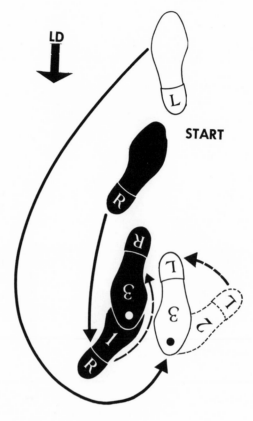

Man

Starting position, weight on left foot, toe pointing out, the right toe behind the left heel.

1. Chest leading, step backward with the right foot, making a quarter turn to the left (1 count).

2. Step with the left foot in back of and across the right foot (1 count).

3. Pivot on the balls of both feet, making another quarter turn to the left, transferring the weight to the right foot; bringing the left foot against the right foot (1 count).

You are now facing in the line of direction.

BACKWARD HALF TURN
VIENNESE WALTZ

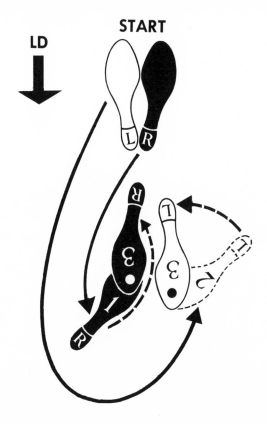

Woman

Backing in the line of direction, feet together, the weight over the ball of the left foot.

1. Chest leading, step backward with the right foot, making a quarter turn to the left (1 count).

2. Step with the left foot in back of and across the right foot (1 count).

3. Pivot on the balls of both feet, making another quarter turn to the left, transferring the weight to the right foot; bringing the left foot against the right foot (1 count).

You are now facing in the line of direction.

BACKWARD HALF TURN
VIENNESE WALTZ

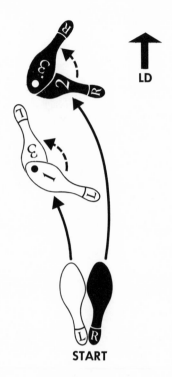

START

(To continue turning, the starting position begins with the weight on the left foot, toe pointing out, the right toe behind the left heel.)

You are now backing in the line of direction.

3. Pivot on the balls of both feet, making another quarter turn to the left, transferring the weight to the left foot as the left heel touches the toe of the right foot (1 count).

2. Follow through with the right foot and take a short step to the right side (1 count).

1. Chest leading, step forward on left foot, making a quarter turn to the left (1 count).

Facing in the line of direction, feet together, the weight over the ball of the right foot.

Woman

FORWARD HALF TURN
VIENNESE WALTZ

14. Samba

HERE is a compact little dance that has come up by way of Brazil. It is light and bouncy and not difficult to learn. Its uneven rhythm gives it a tilting, rocking motion. So keep the knees and ankles loose while practicing.

For those who want a real workout, the samba is ideal.

SAMBA RHYTHM

The music of the samba is in 4/4 ♩ ♩ ♩ ♩ time, the samba rhythm consisting of a dotted quarter note, followed by an eighth note and a half note. Here it is:

$$\frac{4}{4} \quad \text{♩.} \quad \text{♪} \quad \text{♩} \quad |$$

As you can see, the prolonging of the first beat (the dotted quarter note), followed by an eighth note, results in an uneven rhythm. It is this prolonging of the first beat and the sudden shifting to the eighth note that give the characteristic samba rhythm, slow, quick. The adding of the half note gives us slow.

$$\frac{4}{4} \quad \text{♩.} \quad \text{♪} \quad \text{♩} \quad |$$
SLOW   QUICK   SLOW

THE BASIC STEP

The basic step of the samba is done to 4/4 time, and requires one measure of music. The basic rhythm is slow, quick, slow. Keeping the knees in constant motion by bending and straightening, a forward step is taken, slow, followed by a forward step, quick, followed by a "ball change" (transferring the weight from one foot to the other), slow. Here is what the rhythm looks like:

SLOW   QUICK   SLOW

The basic step may be done forward and backward in place, turning in place, progressing up the floor, and from side to side. The basic step is done forward and backward and requires two measures of music. And here it is:

SLOW   QUICK   SLOW   SLOW   QUICK   SLOW

We are going to learn the basic step forward and backward, the left turn, and the shuffle step. Each figure will be described. Some mention will be made of the closed position, the basic step from side to side, the open break, the crossover from side to side, and other variations.

Before progressing to the practice of the basic step, we need to discuss the quick step in the samba. The quick step results in an uneven rhythm, so you will have to be careful to change the weight quickly to correspond with the samba beat. (The tendency in doing the samba is to take an even step on the quick, which is incorrect and results in a two-step rhythm.) So watch out for the quick step. And be sure to dip (bend) in the knees as you step.

As the basic step is taken forward (knees bent), the body tilts back. As the basic step is taken back (knees straight), the body tilts forward. It is this seesaw motion of the samba that makes the dance such fun.

In turning the basic samba step, partners may teeter from side to side. So you see altogether the samba is really a dizzy dance. However, it is still one of the simplest and easiest of all Latin-American dances.

We will now proceed to learn the basic step.

PRACTICING THE BASIC STEP

Man or woman, stand with feet together, the weight over the ball of the right foot.

(Dipping of the knees consists of bending the knees as a step is taken.)

1. Step forward on the left foot, dipping the left knee, slow. (Right knee bends.)

2. Step forward on the ball of the right foot, straightening the knee while transferring the weight, quick.

3. Return the weight to the left foot, dipping in both knees, slow.

You have just done a forward basic step.

You are now standing with bent knees, the hips tilted forward, the weight over the left foot.

To continue:

1. Step back on the right foot, dipping the right knee, slow. (Left knee is bent.)

2. Step back on the ball of the left foot, transferring the weight with bent knee, quick. (Both knees are now bent.)

3. Return the weight to the right foot, straightening both knees, slow.

You have now done a backward basic step.

You are now standing with straight knees, the hips tilted back, the weight over the right foot.

Now practice the basic step continuously, moving forward and backward, calling out slow, quick, slow as you step.

Practice the figure until the rhythm becomes automatic.

SAMBA—CLOSED POSITION
LEFT TURN

Man

(The left turn consists of turning in place, using the forward and backward basic samba step.)

The forward half turn:

1. Chest lead, holding the woman firmly with the right hand while turning left, step forward on the left foot, toe pointing out, dipping the left knee, slow.

2. Step forward on the ball of the right foot, pivoting to the left (the left foot follows through on the pivot), straightening the knee while transferring the weight, quick.

3. Continuing to turn left, return the weight to the left foot, dipping in both knees, slow.

The back half turn:

1. Continuing to turn left, step back on the right foot, toe pointing in, dipping the right knee, slow.

2. Step back on the ball of the left foot, pivoting to the left (the right foot follows through on the pivot), transferring the weight, quick. (Both knees are bent.)

3. Continuing to turn left, return the weight to the right foot, straightening both knees, slow.

Woman

(The left turn consists of turning in place, using the backward and forward basic samba step).

The back half turn:

1. Step back on the right foot, toe pointing in, dipping the right knee, chest turning left, slow.

2. Step back on the ball of the left foot, pivoting to the left (the right foot follows through on the pivot), transferring the weight, quick. (Both knees are bent.)

3. Continuing to turn left, return the weight to the right foot, straightening both knees, slow.

The forward half turn:

1. Continuing to turn left, step forward on the left foot, toe pointing out, dipping the left knee, slow.

2. Step forward on the ball of the right foot, pivoting to the left
   (the left foot follows through on the pivot), straightening the
   knee while transferring the weight, quick.

3. Continuing to turn left, return the weight to the left foot, dipping in both knees, slow.

PRACTICE (VARIATIONS)

Now that you have learned the basic step you may begin to
practice with a partner in closed position, the woman, as usual,
stepping back on the first step. After practicing the closed position in place you may progress to the left turn. For variety, you
might try the basic step from side to side.

For something different try the basic step in open break position. (The man pushes the woman away with the right hand on
the forward basic step, holding her right hand in his left hand.)
The basic step may also be done in an open break from side to
side, the man and woman stepping to the side on slow, and stepping across and back of the supporting foot on quick, returning
the weight to the supporting foot on slow. The crossover from side
to side may be repeated indefinitely.

THE SHUFFLE STEP

Man or woman standing in open break position, step forward
on the outside foot, bending the knees (slow). Dragging the
inside foot slightly backward, straighten the knees (quick); stepping forward on the outside foot, bend the knees (slow). The
figure may now be repeated, beginning with the inside foot.

The samba is such an informal dance and the basic step so
simple that any number of figures may be done in succession.
The turn-under, the man going under his arm, the woman under
her arm, may be done in open break position. And as has been
frequently suggested in learning other dances, try some new combinations.

15. Polka

SOONER or later the polka turns up. And it certainly owes its perennial appeal to its simple, gay rhythm—usually in 2/4 time.

Although there are numerous versions of the polka the "heel and toe and away we go" is by far the most popular as well as the easiest to execute. The more energetic will want to hop and slide. But whichever version is preferred, the lighthearted polka will continue to be popular.

It is as fresh today as it was a hundred years ago and will probably continue to hold its own as an old-time favorite.

BASIC RHYTHM

The basic rhythm of the polka is 2/4 ♪♩ ♪♩ time. In counting the steps to the music, however, we are going to use a 4/4 rhythm ♩ ♩ ♩ ♩

BASIC STEP

The basic polka step consists of a hop, step-close, step-close, and requires one measure of music in 4/4 ♩ ♩ ♩ ♩ time. The hop is taken in place on a sixteenth note (a note added before the first beat). Think of the sixteenth note as an upbeat, calling it "and." The hop is followed immediately by stepping and closing (drawing the foot to the supporting foot and transferring the weight); step-close is repeated, the figure ending on the fourth beat. Here it is:

This is the true polka, and we are going to learn it after we have studied the heel and toe polka with slides. Because of the speed of the polka, the hop-step rhythm is a little more difficult to execute. And as a matter of fact, beginners really prefer the heel and toe combination as a start. Every region has its own version of the polka so that one needn't take the numerous variations too seriously.

We are going to learn first the heel and toe polka combination with slides in skater's position, a variation known as the crossover in skater's position, and the heel and toe combination in closed position. We are also going to include the so-called two-step polka (done without the hop), progressing in closed position; to be followed by the hop-step version, progressing and turning in closed position. Each figure will be described.

Since the man and woman both start on the same foot in skater's position, the steps will be described simultaneously. In assuming the closed position, however, the woman will use the right foot, backing in the customary line of direction. The heel and toe in closed position and the various steps that follow will be described separately.

POLKA–SKATER'S POSITION
(HEEL AND TOE)

Man and Woman

Facing in the line of direction, stand side by side (man's right side against woman's left side), weight over the ball of the right foot; cross arms, joining right hand with right hand, left hand with left hand.

Heel and toe:

1. With toes pointed up, place the left foot diagonally forward, heels touching floor (count 1).

2. Bring the left foot diagonally back, toes touching the floor (count 2).

3. With toes pointed up, place the left foot diagonally forward, heels touching the floor (count 3).

4. Bring the left foot diagonally back, toes touching the floor (count 4).

(The figure requires one measure of music in 4/4 time.)

The slides:

1. Slide diagonally forward on the left foot (count 1). Close the right foot to the left foot, transferring the weight (count and).

2. Slide diagonally forward on the left foot (count 2). Close the right foot to the left foot, transferring the weight (count and).

3. Slide diagonally forward on the left foot (count 3). Close the right foot to the left foot, transferring the weight (count and).

4. Slide diagonally forward on the left foot (count 4). The right foot follows through (count and).

(The figure requires one measure of music in 4/4 time.)

The entire figure (the heel and toe and slides) may now be repeated to the right, beginning with the right foot.

POLKA—SKATER'S POSITION
(VARIATION)
THE CROSSOVER

Man and Woman

The crossover consists of the man switching the woman from his right side over to his left side.

Facing in the line of direction, the woman's left shoulder against the man's right shoulder, the hands clasped vertically at shoulder level, the weight over the ball of the right foot.

1. Starting with the left foot, do the heel and toe combination twice in place (count 4).

2. Slide diagonally forward on the left foot three times, closing with the right foot (count 3).

3. Step diagonally forward on the left foot (count 1), while transferring the woman quickly from the right shoulder to the left shoulder, the woman stepping across and in front of the man.

(Two measures of music in 4/4 time are required for the entire figure.)

The woman now has her right shoulder against the man's left shoulder.

The entire figure (the heel and toe and slides) may now be repeated to the right, beginning with the right foot.

POLKA–CLOSED POSITION
(HEEL AND TOE)

Man

In the heel and toe and slide combination in closed position the man clasps the woman at the waist.

Facing in the line of direction, feet together, the weight over the ball of the right foot.

Heel and toe:

1. With toe pointed up, place the left foot diagonally to the side, the heel touching the floor (count 1).

2. Bring the left foot diagonally back, the toe touching the floor (count 2).

3. With toe pointed up, place the left foot diagonally to the side, the heel touching the floor (count 3).

4. Bring the left foot diagonally back, the toe touching the floor (count 4).

(The figure requires one measure of music in 4/4 time.)

The slides:

1. Slide diagonally forward on the left foot (count 1). Close the right foot to the left foot, transferring the weight (count and).

2. Slide diagonally forward on the left foot (count 2). Close the right foot to the left foot, transferring the weight (count and).

3. Slide diagonally forward on the left foot (count 3). Close the right foot to the left foot, transferring the weight (count and).

4. Slide diagonally forward on the left foot (count 4). The right foot follows through (count and).

(The figure requires one measure of music in 4/4 time.)

The entire figure (the heel and toe and slides) may now be repeated to the right, beginning with the right foot.

POLKA—CLOSED POSITION
(HEEL AND TOE)

Woman

In the heel and toe and slide combination in closed position the woman places her hands on the man's shoulders.

Backing in the line of direction, feet together, the weight over the ball of the left foot.

Heel and toe:

1. With toe pointed up, place the right foot diagonally to the side, the heel touching the floor (count 1).

2. Bring the right foot diagonally back, the toe touching the floor (count 2).

3. With toe pointed up, place the right foot diagonally to the side, the heel touching the floor (count 3).

4. Bring the right foot diagonally back, the toe touching the floor (count 4).

(The figure requires one measure of music in 4/4 time.)

The slides:

1. Slide back diagonally on the right foot (count 1). Close the left foot to the right foot, transferring the weight (count and).

2. Slide back diagonally on the right foot (count 2). Close the left foot to the right foot, transferring the weight (count and).

3. Slide back diagonally on the right foot (count 3). Close the left foot to the right foot, transferring the weight (count and).

4. Slide back diagonally on the right foot (count 4). The left foot follows through (count and).

(The figure requires one measure of music in 4/4 time.)

The entire figure (the heel and toe and slides) may now be repeated to the left, beginning with the left foot.

POLKA—CLOSED POSITION
(WITHOUT HOP)

Man

Facing in the line of direction, feet together, the weight over the ball of the right foot.

1. Step diagonally forward on the left foot (count 1). Close the right foot to the left foot, transferring the weight (count and).

2. Step diagonally forward on the left foot (count 2). The right foot follows through (count and).

3. Step diagonally forward on the right foot (count 3). Close the left foot to the right foot, transferring the weight (count and).

4. Step diagonally forward on the right foot (count 4). The left foot follows through (count and).

(You have just completed a polka step to the left and to the right. The figure requires one measure of music in 4/4 time.)

The entire figure may now be repeated.

Woman

Backing in the line of direction, feet together, the weight over the ball of the left foot.

1. Step back diagonally on the right foot (count 1). Close the left foot to the right foot, transferring the weight (count and).

2. Step back diagonally on the right foot (count 2). The left foot follows through (count and).

3. Step back diagonally on the left foot (count 3). Close the right foot to the left foot, transferring the weight (count and).

4. Step back diagonally on the left foot (count 4). The right foot follows through (count and).

(You have just completed a polka step to the right and to the left. The figure requires one measure of music in 4/4 time.)

The entire figure may now be repeated.

POLKA–CLOSED POSITION
(WITH HOP)

Man

Facing in the line of direction, feet together, the weight over the ball of the right foot.

Hopping on the right foot and bending the left knee (count and):

1. Step diagonally forward on the left foot (count 1).

2. Close the right foot to the left foot, transferring the weight (count 2).

3. Step diagonally forward on the left foot (count 3).

4. The right foot follows through (count 4).

Hopping on the left foot and bending the right knee (count and):

1. Step diagonally forward on the right foot (count 1).

2. Close the left foot to the right foot, transferring the weight (count 2).

3. Step diagonally forward on the right foot (count 3).

4. The left foot follows through (count 4).

(You have just completed a polka step to the left and to the right. The figure requires two measures of music in 4/4 time.)

The entire figure may now be repeated.

POLKA—CLOSED POSITION
(WITH HOP)

Woman

Backing in the line of direction, feet together, the weight over the ball of the left foot.

Hopping on the left foot and bending the right knee (count and):

1. Step back diagonally on the right foot (count 1).

2. Close the left foot to the right foot, transferring the weight (count 2).

3. Step back diagonally on the right foot (count 3).

4. The left foot follows through (count 4).

Hopping on the right foot and bending the left knee (count and):

1. Step back diagonally on the left foot (count 1).

2. Close the right foot to the left foot, transferring the weight (count 2).

3. Step back diagonally on the left foot (count 3).

4. The right foot follows through (count 4).

(You have just completed a polka step to the right and to the left. The figure requires two measures of music in 4/4 time.)

The entire figure may now be repeated.

POLKA—CLOSED POSITION
TURN
(WITH HOP)

Man

The polka turn consists of doing a half right turn in the line of direction and continuing to the right with another half right turn.

Facing in the line of direction, stand with feet together, the weight over the ball of the right foot.

Hopping on the right foot while turning to the right, and bending the left knee (count and):

1. Step to the side on the left foot (count 1).

2. Close the right foot to the left foot, transferring the weight (count 2).

3. Continuing to turn right, step back on the left foot (count 3).

4. The right foot follows through (count 4).

Hop on the left foot, bending the right knee (count and):

1. Step to the side on the right foot (count 1).

2. Close the left foot to the right foot, transferring the weight (count 2).

3. Continuing to turn right, step forward on the right foot (count 3).

4. The left foot follows through (count 4).

(The figure requires two measures of music in 4/4 time.)

POLKA—CLOSED POSITION
TURN
(WITH HOP)

Woman

The polka turn consists of doing a half right turn, backing in the line of direction and continuing to the right with another half right turn.

Backing in the line of direction, stand with feet together, the weight over the ball of the left foot.

Hopping on the left foot while turning right, and bending the right knee (count and):

1. Step to the side on the right foot (count 1).

2. Close the left foot to the right foot, transferring the weight (count 2).

3. Continuing to turn right, step forward on the right foot (count 3).

4. The left foot follows through (count 4).

Hop on the right foot, bending the left knee (count and):

1. Step to the side on the left foot (count 1).

2. Close the right foot to the left foot, transferring the weight (count 2).

3. Continuing to turn right, step back on the left foot (count 3).

4. The right foot follows through (count 4).

(The figure requires two measures of music in 4/4 time.)

PRACTICE

Although the polka, in closed position, may be done with the customary clasp, the waltz, for example, it is a little safer while doing the polka, for the man to clasp the woman's waist, the woman clasping the man's shoulders. And in order to get good leverage, while turning, partners should lean away from each other.

In changing direction, partners should look in the new direction before beginning the following figure. (You do have to see where you are going, you know.) And because of the speed with which one moves while dancing the polka, one will have to watch out for other couples on the floor to avoid collisions.

VARIATIONS

Now that you have learned the heel and toe, the slide, and the basic polka steps in the skater's and the closed position, try some other variations. For instance, in addition to doing the skater's position with the crossover, which has been described, you might try the throw-over (tossing the woman from the right side to the left side). See pages 154–56.

The polka step (without the hop) may also be varied by turning in closed position. And at intervals the woman may turn under her right arm. And for something even more giddy, the man may polka in place while swinging the woman around him with his right arm overhead, the woman's left hand clasped in his right hand.

For those who really get wound up doing the polka, there is a four-hand variation. Two couples in open position join inside hands, the head couple (the couple in front) joining outside hands with the couple behind while progressing in the line of direction. At any moment the head couple may back up under the inside arms of the couple behind, the two couples continuing to progress in the line of direction. From here on you may try your own variations.

16. Calypso

AT first glance, it would seem as though there were almost as many versions of the dance called Calypso as there are islands in the Caribbean. However, despite the dazzling variety of steps and figures being constantly innovated, the easygoing Calypso is really quite simple. Once you have mastered the basic movement —which is characteristic of most Caribbean dances—you will find yourself improvising a variety of steps to the amusing, spicy lyrics of the Calypso bands.

The basic movement consists of placing the foot flat against the floor (knee bent), the weight following as the step is taken. (For a complete analysis of the step, see pages 66 and 67—the rumba movement.) We will refer to this movement in the descriptive material for the basic step as "place-step."

In addition to the place-step, however, the Calypso has a distinctive hip movement that gives it its particular flavor. This consists of pushing up into the hip.

THE BASIC RHYTHM

The basic rhythm of the Calypso is in 2/4 ♩ ♩ time. In counting the steps to the music, however, we are going to use a 4/4 rhythm.

THE BASIC STEP

The basic step consists of two quick place-steps and one slow place-step with an accent in the hip which is done on the fourth count of a 4/4 measure. Here is what it looks like:

PLACE — STEP   PLACE — STEP   PLACE —— STEP — HIP

We are going to learn the basic step sideward, forward, and backward. From here we will progress to the right turn-under, the open position, and back to back. Each figure will be described.

Later we will describe the Calypso Walk and include numerous variations. Some mention will be made regarding the Charleston rhythm and the "banana step."

We are now ready to proceed with the basic step.

CALYPSO
SIDEWARD BASIC STEP

Man

Left side:

Stand in closed position, feet together, the weight over the right foot.

1. Place-step to the left side on the left foot (count 1).

2. Place-step to the left side on the right foot (count 2).

3. Continuing to the left side, place the left foot, no weight (count 3).

4. Transferring the weight to the left foot, push up into the left hip, raising the left heel slightly (count 4).

Right side:

1. Place-step to the right side on the right foot (count 1).

2. Place-step to the right side on the left foot (count 2).

3. Continuing to the right side, place the right foot, no weight (count 3).

4. Transferring the weight to the right foot, push up into the right hip, raising the right heel slightly (count 4).

CALYPSO
SIDEWARD BASIC STEP

Woman

Right side:

Stand in closed position, feet together, the weight over the left foot.

1. Place-step to the right side on the right foot (count 1).

2. Place-step to the right side on the left foot (count 2).

3. Continuing to the right side, place the right foot, no weight (count 3).

4. Transferring the weight to the right foot, push up into the right hip, raising the right heel slightly (count 4).

Left side:

1. Place-step to the left side on the left foot (count 1).

2. Place-step to the left side on the right foot (count 2).

3. Continuing to the left side, place the left foot, no weight (count 3).

4. Transferring the weight to the left foot, push up into the left hip, raising the left heel slightly (count 4).

CALYPSO
FORWARD BASIC STEP

Man

Stand in closed position, feet together, the weight over the right foot.

1. Place-step forward on the left foot (count 1).
2. Place-step forward on the right foot (count 2).
3. Continuing, place the left foot forward (count 3).
4. Transferring the weight to the left foot, push up into the left hip, raising the left heel slightly (count 4).

The figure may now be repeated, beginning with the right foot.

CALYPSO
BACK BASIC STEP

Woman

Stand in closed position, feet together, the weight over the left foot.

1. Place-step backward on the right foot (count 1).
2. Place-step backward on the left foot (count 2).
3. Continuing, place the right foot backward (count 3).
4. Transferring the weight to the right foot, push up into the right hip, raising the right heel slightly (count 4).

The figure may now be repeated, beginning with the left foot.

NOTE: At all times, the foot should be placed flat on the floor while stepping backward.

RIGHT TURN-UNDER

Man

Starting in a closed position, the man takes a basic step to the left followed by a basic step to the right. On the fourth count of the basic step to the right, the man raises the woman's right arm and pushes the left side of the woman's torso with his right hand in preparation for the right turn-under.

The man takes two basic steps in place as the woman circles in front of him, resuming the closed position.

RIGHT TURN-UNDER

Woman

Starting in closed position, the woman takes a basic step to the right followed by a basic step to the left. On the fourth count of the basic step to the left, the woman pivots on her left foot a quarter of a turn to the right, as the man raises her right arm in preparation for the right turn-under.

Turning under her right arm, the woman takes two forward basic steps, describing a circle in front of the man, resuming the closed position.

OPEN POSITION

Man

Starting in closed position, sideward in the line of direction, the man takes one basic step to the left, followed by a basic step to the right. On the fourth count of the basic step to the right, the man pivots on his right foot a quarter of a turn to the left, releasing the woman's right hand and taking her left hand in his right hand. He is now in open position.

Moving forward in the line of direction, the man takes two basic steps. On the fourth count of the second basic step, the man pivots on his right foot a quarter of a turn to his right, resuming the closed position.

We have described the figure in open position with two basic steps forward. The figure can also be done with any *even* number of basic steps.

OPEN POSITION

Woman

Starting in closed position, sideward in the line of direction, the woman takes one basic step to the right, followed by a basic step to the left. On the fourth count of the basic step to the left, the woman pivots on her left foot a quarter of a turn to the right, the man releasing her right hand and taking her left hand. She is now in open position.

Moving forward in the line of direction, the woman takes two basic steps. On the fourth count of the second basic step, the woman pivots on her left foot a quarter of a turn to the left, resuming the closed position.

We have described the figure in open position with two basic steps forward. The figure can also be done with any *even* number of basic steps.

BACK TO BACK

Man

Standing sideward in the line of direction facing the woman, holding her left hand in his right hand, the man takes one basic step to the left. On the fourth count of the basic step, the man pivots on his left foot a half turn to the left. He is now back to back with his partner.

From the back-to-back position, the man takes a basic step to the right. On the fourth count, the man pivots on his right foot a half turn to the right. He is now facing his partner.

The figure may be repeated several times, the man continuing to hold the woman's left hand in his right hand.

BACK TO BACK

Woman

Standing sideward in the line of direction facing the man, with her left hand in his right hand, the woman takes one basic step to the right. On the fourth count of the basic step, the woman pivots on her right foot a half turn to the right. She is now back to back with her partner.

From the back-to-back position, the woman takes a basic step to the left. On the fourth count, the woman pivots on her left foot a half turn to the left. She is now facing her partner.

The figure may be repeated several times, the woman keeping her left hand in the man's right hand.

PRACTICE (VARIATIONS)

Having learned to use the basic step in the preceding figures, you will find it interesting to add some new figures. The basic step, for example, can be turned in place to the left, or partners may even turn in place in opposite directions—the man turning to the left, the woman turning to the right.

We have described the open position with the woman on the man's right side. The figure can also be done with the woman on the man's left side. Starting in closed position, the man pushes the woman with his right hand over to his left side on a forward basic step, into open position.

And now, it is time to proceed to the Calypso Walk.

THE CALYPSO WALK

(Carnival Walk)

The Calypso Walk—popularly known as the Carnival Walk—is essentially a step used in processions at festival time. The step consists of placing or stamping the foot with knee bent while pushing up into the *other* hip. (See page 212.)

In addition to using the Calypso Walk in a procession, the step is also used in regular dance positions—for example, closed, open, or back-to-back position. Here is how we do the Calypso Walk. Stand with feet together, the weight over the right foot.

Place or stamp forward with the left foot while pushing up into the right hip. Transfer the weight to the left foot (step). Place or stamp forward with the right foot while pushing up into the left hip. Transfer the weight to the right foot (step). Here is what the rhythm looks like:

PLACE   STEP   PLACE   STEP

(PUSH HIP)   (PUSH HIP)

PRACTICE (VARIATIONS)

Having learned the walk you are now ready to practice with a partner in closed position. The step may be done forward and backward, or walking in a circle. For variety, a turn may be done in place. Moving in opposite directions, the man turns to his left while the woman turns to her right. Occasionally, a right turn-under or left turn-under can be inserted, the man marking time in place while the woman circles in front of her partner.

From here you may progress to the open position by taking three steps forward in the line of direction, and turning on the fourth step into open position. Incidentally, we suggest taking four walking steps in any of the preceding figures. You will also find it helpful to take four walking steps in closed position *between* the various figures. And try some combinations of your own.

Before leaving the Calypso Walk, we would like to mention an intriguing variation of the step that consists of flexing the knee twice and stepping, or stamping the foot twice and stepping. This doubling of the movement can be used in all of the figures that have been previously described—perhaps the most amusing being the back-to-back figure. Again, we suggest practicing four steps to a figure.

And finally, the more advanced dancer will enjoy doing the under-the-arch figure. Here is how it is done. Partners facing each other, holding both hands, the man raises the woman's right arm, forming an arch. Partners turn under the arch, finishing back to back. The man now releases the woman's left hand, circling her to her right in front of him as he marks time in place. The figure requires four steps.

THE CHARLESTON RHYTHM

Wouldn't you like to do something entirely different to the Calypso music? Then try the Charleston! You can do the point step forward and back, the twist step (without the kicks), or the stamp. (For a complete analysis of the Charleston, see pages 136 through 145.) Unlike the more strenuous Charleston, however, the Calypso style is done in a smooth, easygoing manner—the knees remaining flexed with the feet more or less parallel with the floor.

Before we wind up the Calypso, we would like to include a variation known as the "banana step." It consists of pointing with the heel to the side, tilting the body back, stepping in place, bending the knees, and pivoting to the other side on the supporting foot. From here, you are on your own.

17. Square Dance

FOR downright fun and sociability nothing can equal a square dance. It is the one occasion that gives everybody a chance to get in the act. And it is as typically American as our free way of life.

Like any social skill, however, that involves participation with other people, some preliminary knowledge is necessary. And for the beginner in square dancing knowledge and practice of the basic figures are an absolute must. Remember, square dancing really moves along, so it is important for you to know your own part in order to keep up with the set (four couples). It isn't enough to know the figures. One must be able to execute them as rapidly as the caller reels them off.

THE BASIC FIGURES

A Set

A set consists of four couples who face the center of the square. Each man stands with the woman at his right side. The head couple at home base stand with their backs to the caller.

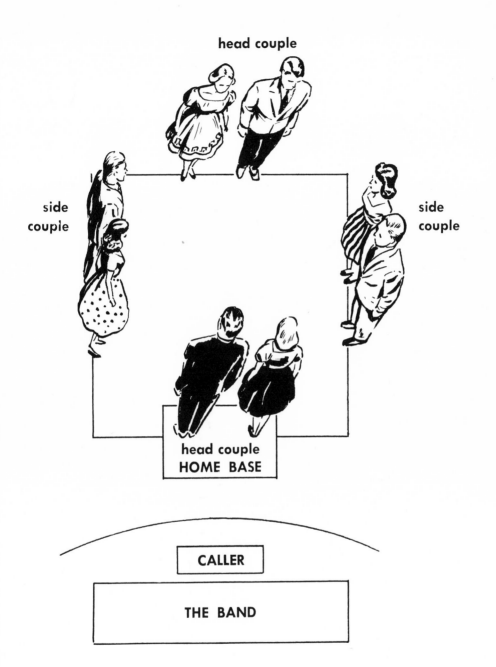

head couple

side couple

side couple

head couple
HOME BASE

CALLER

THE BAND

Corners

For the man—the lady on your left is your corner.
For the woman—the gent on your right is your corner.

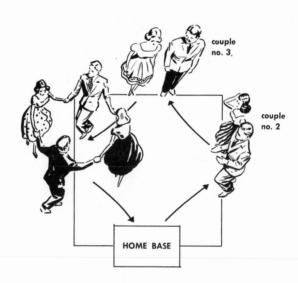

How to Progress in a Set

The word progress in a set means to go visiting. Couples travel in a counterclockwise direction.

Couple number one begin the figure. They move to the right to visit couple number two. After dancing with couple number two, couple number one move on to couple number three. (Couple number two remain in place.) The same procedure is followed with couples number three and four. After dancing with couple number four couple number one return to the home base.

Each couple in turn go visiting, progressing around the set until the dance has been completed.

Honor Your Partner

Honor your partner means to bow to your partner.

The man turns toward his right, bending slightly from the waist as he bows to his partner.

The woman turns toward her left and curtsies to her partner. A curtsy consists of stepping on the left foot, bending the left knee while the right toe is tucked behind the left heel.

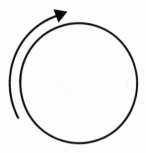

Eight Hands Around

Eight hands around is the call for circling to the left. The four couples join hands and walk around clockwise.

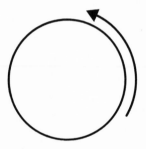

Back the Other Way

Back the other way means to circle right. The four couples reverse the direction, walking counterclockwise.

Swing Your Partner

Swing your partner, as the call implies, means to turn with your partner in one spot in a clockwise direction.

POSITION OF THE MAN AND WOMAN

Facing in opposite directions—right side to right side, and with the feet slightly apart, stand with the weight forward on the right foot, outside edge of soles almost touching. The right

arm circles the woman's waist. The left hand clasps the woman's
right hand with the arms extended in a curve slightly below
shoulder level. The woman's left hand rests on the man's right
shoulder.

HOW TO SWING YOUR PARTNER—MAN AND WOMAN

Stand with the weight forward on the right foot. Step slightly
forward on the ball of the left foot, raise the right heel, and pivot
(turn) on the ball of the right foot; lower the right heel.

Repeat—continuing to push with the left foot while pivoting firmly on the ball of the right foot, and you will have no difficulty in turning on one spot. Lean away slightly from each other
as you turn and you will find it easier to maintain your balance.

Allemande Left

Allemande left is a left-hand turn with corners.

MAN AND WOMAN

Face your corner. Clasp left hands, walk around counterclockwise making a complete turn, return to place.

Grand Right and Left

The men walk in a circle, counterclockwise, the women walk clockwise, each clasping hands as they meet.

HOW TO DO IT

Partners face each other, clasp right hands, and walking past each other, each gives the left hand to the next person; the right hand to the next, the left hand to the next until each returns to his original place.

Promenade

Promenade means to walk around the set.

MAN AND WOMAN

Facing in a counterclockwise direction, standing side by side, cross arms, joining right hand with right hand, left hand with left hand (skater's position), and march once around the set until you reach your original place.

PRACTICE

There's bound to be a square-dance enthusiast among your friends who can go over the basic calls with you. Better still, get a group together and form a set and walk through the figures. It's more fun that way and may even provide an opportunity for some amateur to do a little calling on his own. And be sure to wear light, porous clothing and comfortable shoes while you practice.

THE MUSIC

The customary music for square dancing is jigs and reels—usually in 2/4 ♪ ♩ ♪ ♩ or 6/8 ♪ ♪ ♩ ♪ ♪ ♩ time. The music accompanies the calls. Frequently about eight measures of music are played as the caller announces the dance. And that will be your signal to join a set.

Your cue for starting on time will be given by the caller about two measures in advance. By listening to the caller as you dance, you will automatically get through on time without having to count the beats in the music. Keep alert to the calls and you will be dancing in perfect rhythm to the music.

USING ADDITIONAL FIGURES

Having learned the basic figures that have just been described, you are now ready to go out on the floor and participate in any of the figures that go to make up a square dance. The following are among the most popular with the average person: "Birdie in the Cage," "Chase the Rabbit," "Buffalo Boys," "Around That Couple and Take a Peek," "Dive for the Oyster," "The Basket," "The Star."

The easiest way to learn these figures is to get right in and do them. Some familiarity, however, with a square-dance book or record album—before the dance—can help considerably to get you through. Whatever you do, practice.

And finally, for the dancer who is really good, here are a few pointers which should enable even him to become more expert.

Wait for the caller.

If you get behind on a call, skip that figure and catch up with the others.

(The main thing is to stay with the caller.)

If you get ahead, wait in place for the next figure.

If you are a beginner, stick to side couples.

(You can observe the head couple perform first.)

Stay in a set until the caller is through.

ORGANIZING A SQUARE DANCE

You should decide—right from the start—whether you are going to aim for a big jamboree or a small gathering. The number of sets will determine the size of the hall and the setup in the choice of caller and music.

The Caller

The caller is of first importance, for in addition to calling he may have to teach the figures and act as master of ceremonies. It is his job to hold the groups together and direct the band. However, if you can't budget for a professional caller and band, the next best thing is to settle for a person in the community who can handle the calls. And make no mistake—experienced amateur callers can do a first-rate job. The caller will need, as a basic, minimum requirement, a pianist to accompany the calls. If you are planning for more than thirty-two people (four sets) it will be necessary to have a microphone so that the caller can be heard.

The Music

The ideal setup for any square dance is to have live calling and music, but if that is not practicable, recorded music and calls can be used. Beginners, however, will have some difficulty in following records on account of the speed of the calls and a certain amount of acoustical distortion. If you are planning for a large gathering amplifiers will have to be used. The great advantage of hiring a caller and musician is that the responsibility for running the program is in their hands. But if you are planning the program and records are to be used, some care will have to be exercised in the choice of calls.

Records

You will need an all-around collection of slow, fast, easy, and difficult calls to keep everyone happy. And it will be wise to have one set (four couples) familiarize themselves with the calls on the records for demonstration purposes—before the dance. Much time and effort can be saved at the dance if one set can walk through the different figures. And the process of helping beginners on the floor can be speeded up if the more experienced couples can join the less experienced sets.

The Dances

Start off with slow, easy dances for warming up. After the groups have gone into action they can progress to the faster, more difficult calls. And for variety an occasional circle or longways dance can be inserted; for example, the Virginia reel.

Occasionally a request is made for round dancing, so it might be wise to have a collection of waltzes, foxtrots, and polkas on hand. Round dances, however, should be used sparingly. The purpose of a square dance, after all, is to give everyone a chance to dance with his friends and neighbors. And if round dances are introduced too frequently the dancers tend to pair off in couples.

After you have organized your first square dance you will find the going easy. And you will be amply rewarded by the results—good fellowship and a sense of belonging through sharing. This is the spirit of the American square dance!

18. Public Dance

A PUBLIC dance is a complicated affair, so it will be necessary to go into some detail. A dance doesn't run itself, and unless it is well organized it will fall apart. You can be sure that any dance you attended that was really successful meant plenty of hard work on the part of the committees as well as zip and imagination.

There are two aspects to consider in setting up any good dance. First, the business or organizational end, which forms the backbone for the "behind the scene" work. Second, the social aspect—choosing a social director, hostesses, ushers, etc. And both of these objectives must dovetail for a dance to run smoothly.

As soon as you have decided on the kind of dance you will want, begin at once to appoint your committees.

ORGANIZATION COMMITTEES

Tickets

There is no more important aspect in organizing a dance than the handling of tickets. It is an exacting job, so some care will have to be exercised in choosing the members for such a committee. Tickets will have to be printed, distributed, and collected upon admission. And a record should be kept of the entire sale of tickets.

Before tickets are printed, a committee member should contact the local Collector of Internal Revenue to obtain information about the Federal Admissions Tax and to check the requirements for claiming a tax exemption. If all the proceeds of a dance are to go exclusively toward a benefit, a church for example, an exemption may be claimed. Otherwise, an admissions tax will have to be paid in order to comply with the regulations for the Federal tax law.

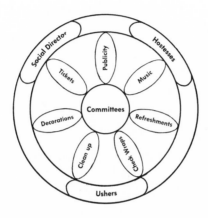

MUSIC

Hiring a Band

If you are going to hire a band it will be necessary for the committee to shop around and get estimates. And keep in mind the style of the music the band plays since music is such an integral part of the dance.

Using Records

It is good planning to have at least one or two persons to take care of the record situation. One member of the committee should be appointed to run the machine and possibly another to list the choice of records to be used. Finally, the machine and record collection should be checked before the dance gets under way.

DECORATION

It takes more than a flair for decorating for people to function as a committee. Materials will have to be budgeted for and measurements taken of both the room and tables before purchases are made. And if refreshments are to be served, utensils and accessories should be provided by the decoration committee.

REFRESHMENTS

The committee members should decide what refreshments are suitable. If homemade snacks and punch are not to be provided, it will be necessary to budget for outside refreshments and to order well in advance. A few members should be appointed to serve refreshments and to keep supplies replenished.

CHECKING WRAPS

The committee should know in advance what equipment is available for disposing of wraps. If a checking system is to be used, details such as check stubs, gratuities, etc., should also be arranged for. It is good planning to have the same members check out guests' wraps as well as in.

CLEANUP

No committee performs a more vital function than the cleanup squad. So appoint responsible members with a flair for housekeeping. And try to recruit a member of the decoration committee to help take down decorations before cleaning up.

PUBLICITY

Every effort should be made to co-ordinate the various activities of the members of the committee. In addition to handling a mailing list the members may have to handle distribution of posters, printed or mimeographed announcements. And a follow-up group should see that announcements are posted. Every means should be used to publicize the dance including the local papers and word of mouth. Talk about it! In addition, each member of the committee should be responsible for disposing of a certain amount of tickets. And if an advertising bill has to be met one person should be appointed to handle it.

Sounds like a tall order, doesn't it, but it's the publicity and public relations job that sells a dance. Extra effort may mean the difference between a mediocre or a completely successful affair.

SOCIAL COMMITTEE

Although the size of a dance determines how specialized the functions are of the various members of a social committee, the members should be chosen for their social assets—tact, a sense of humor, and a talent for getting along with other people. Hostesses and ushers will be required to keep the dance running smoothly, and a good social director is a must!

A social director should know at a glance what is going on every minute. The most important asset is a sense of timing. Lightning decisions will have to be made at any moment to keep things moving. And mixers and party games will have to be run during the slack periods at a good, snappy pace in order to hold the group together. Prizes and "props" such as tickets for lucky-number dances should be organized in advance. The director will also have to know when refreshments should be served. Altogether, it is an exacting job, so considerable thought should be given to the choosing of a social director.

The chief function of hostesses and ushers is to receive guests, effect introductions, and smooth over difficult situations. By being in circulation on the floor at all times, they become an integral part of the dance. They should also be ready to be on call at any time the social director may need them. Ushers acting as "stags" should keep women without partners in circulation. However, relief of assisting stags should be provided for.

CHURCH DANCE

One of the nicest things about a church dance is the opportunity it provides for meeting friends and neighbors from other churches. The church dance need not be confined to close friends, as is so often the case, but can be an excuse for rounding out one's social life.

After a committee has been formed a member should contact the pastor or his secretary for permission to use the church. In setting a date the church calendar should be checked so as to avoid overlapping with other activities including preparations for the dance. The sexton should be consulted as to use of church equipment. And if heavy demands are to be made on his time, some form of gratuity should be provided. Saturday nights should be avoided so as not to conflict with preparations for Sunday services. Finally, some member of the committee should be appointed to express appreciation for the privilege of using the church—either verbally or through a written note.

DINNER OR SUPPER DANCE

Since both the dinner and supper dance fall under the classification of dining out, the procedure for either will vary little.

The dinner dance is usually scheduled from 6 to 10:30 P.M. The supper dance from 10:30 P.M.

Inquiry should be made as to the type of orchestra, entertainment, time of show, cover charge (if any), and menu, when a reservation is made. The date and hour of arrival should be given to reservation clerk as well as the number of guests to be provided for. Dress is optional.

19. Grand March

WE now arrive at the grand march—the high spot of any dance. We are going to discuss the leader's role in organizing a grand march and describe fully the various formations in the following order: platoons, the serpentine, the arch, and tunneling. Some mention will be made about the star formation.

It is not necessary for a leader to use the grand march formations in the order in which they will be described in the following section. A leader should feel perfectly free at any moment to make changes in the progression of the formations. And to add zest to a dance, some new formations should be tried.

PRACTICING THE GRAND MARCH

The first thing a grand march calls for is a good leader. Just as a band needs a drum major to keep time, a grand march requires a leader who can call out and direct the various figures. The grand march is after all the climax of any social affair so everyone will want to be in it. And what could be more fun than locking arms with one's friends and just marching down the floor to a good, snappy tune?

Before the leader announces the grand march to the guests a couple should be ready to head up the march. The band is informed in advance so that it is ready to start. As soon as the leader has announced the grand march the band starts warming

front of room

up, the head couple rise and march in a circle, counterclockwise, and the guests follow behind. The leader at this point is in the center of the floor to hold the group together and to direct the head couple for the next figure.

From now on the leader takes over, and his ability to anticipate the various calls and call them out clearly will determine the success of the march.

Since the platoon formation—marching abreast—is the most spontaneous and natural way to continue the march, the leader will probably start off in the traditional way—with platoons. All such formations will shape up or begin at the back of the room although the call will have been given by the leader to the head couple at the front, where the lines usually divide to prepare for the following figure. Whether the leader prefers to remain at the front in one spot and call out the figure or march backward each time in front of the head couple is of little importance. The main thing is for the head couple to hear the next figure and keep alert to the various changes in calls. Any hesitancy on the part of the head couple will throw off the couples behind and result in confusion. And a grand march that doesn't have a crisp, snappy look isn't worth the effort. So here we go!

PLATOONS

Figure I

The leader calls to the head couple, "Down the center and divide." As the head couple, the line following, reach the center of the back of the room they make a sharp left turn, march forward, and divide at the front of the room, the women turning right, the men turning left, the lines proceeding toward the back wall.

back of room

front of room

Figure II

Continuing in single file up the room, the head couple meet
in the center, clasp arms, and march down the floor, couples
following two abreast. On reaching the front of the room, the
head couple turn right, the second couple in line turn left, each
couple alternating right and left, the lines proceeding toward the
back wall.

back of room

front of room

Figure III

Continuing in two columns up the room, the head couples meet in the center, clasp arms, and march down the floor, four abreast, couples following, and divide at the bottom, the head couple on the right turning right, the head couple on the left turning left, the line following, couples in turn alternating right and left, the lines proceeding toward the back wall.

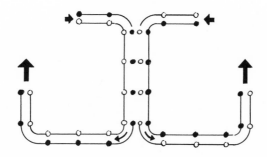

Figure IV

Continuing in two columns up the room, the head couples meet in the center, clasp arms, and march down the floor, four abreast, couples following. On reaching the front of the room, the head couples turn right, the couples in the second line turn left, the line following, couples alternating right and left, the lines proceeding toward the back wall.

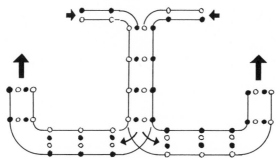

Figure V

Continuing in two columns up the room, the head couples meet in the center, clasp arms, and march down the floor, eight abreast, the lines following, and divide at the bottom, the two head couples on the right turning right, the two head couples on the left turning left, the line following, dividing right and left, the lines proceeding toward the back wall.

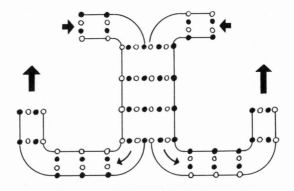

Figure VI

Continuing in two columns up the room, the head couples meet in the center, clasp arms, and march down the floor, eight abreast, the line following. On reaching the front of the room, the four head couples turn right, the couples in the second line turn left, each line following, alternating right and left, the lines proceeding toward the back wall.

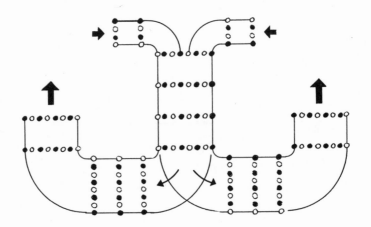

Now that you have become familiar with the platoon formations, you may continue to build up even longer lines. For example, continuing from the end of Figure VI, in which two columns, eight abreast, are marching up the room, the head couples may meet in the center, clasp arms, and march down the floor, sixteen abreast, the lines following, to divide at the bottom, the eight head couples turning right, the couples in the second line turning left, each line following, alternating right and left, the lines proceeding toward the back wall.

Thirty-two people may march abreast down the floor by repeating the procedure of meeting at the back wall, clasping arms and marching forward.

As a matter of fact, any number of persons may march abreast, in couples, but the lines will become unwieldy in dividing and turning if more than thirty-two are attempted. At all times, the couples initiating the turns will have to mark time while turning to allow time for the outer couples in line to make the turn. The couples toward the center of the turn will have to take small steps, the couples next, graduating the length of their stride, the outermost couples taking the longest stride. (Remember the principle of spokes radiating from the hub of a wheel.)

And finally, in turning, the elbows should be kept close to the body in a firm clasp, to help keep the lines closely knit.

GRAND MARCH FORMATIONS

Serpentine

The serpentine consists of a leader with the line following him walking back and forth between the lines of a platoon formation, picking up a new line each time that line is passed.

The serpentine is an excellent figure to have up your sleeve for breaking up the platoon formation. However enthusiastic couples may feel while marching, even a grand march must end sometime! And the serpentine figure is the solution.

Starting with a platoon formation, hands joined, the leader makes a sharp turn to his left, and drawing the line with him, walks across in front of the second line until he reaches the end person, makes a sharp turn to his right, and continuing, walks across in front of the third line. The leader, the line following, now makes a sharp turn to his left as he passes the end man of the third line, and continues forward across in front of the fourth line (Figure A). As the end woman of line number one passes the end man of line number two she joins her right hand in his left hand, thus joining the two lines (Figure B).

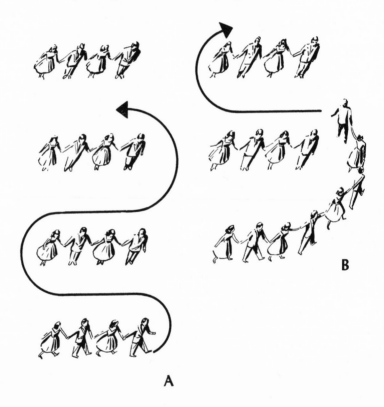

A

B

The leader, continuing to draw the line with him, now makes a sharp turn to the right while passing the end woman of line number four, and continues across in front of line number five. In the meantime the end woman of line number two, in passing, has picked up the end man of line number three. (See Figure C.)

The leader continues to draw the line through the remaining formations, the end woman each time, in passing, picking up the end man of the line which has just been passed.

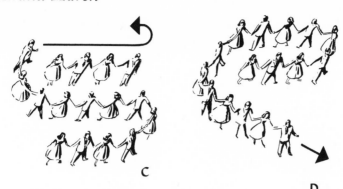

C

D

Eventually all the lines will be picked up as the leader, the line following, moves back and forth, the entire group following in single file in a counterclockwise direction (Figure D).

Arch

Arching (sometimes called the "arbor") consists of couples facing in opposite lines, raising the arms, and joining hands, thus forming an arch.

There are two methods of arching—one, in which all the couples form an arch simultaneously, and two, in which each couple arch separately. We are going to describe the latter figure —number two.

Partners stand in opposite lines, facing each other. Couple number one (the head couple) form an arch (Figure A) and couple number two duck under to the opposite side of couple number one.

Couple number one and two form an arch, and couple number three duck under the arch (Figure B), passing through to the opposite side of couple number two.

Couples number one, two, and three form an arch, and couple number four duck under, passing through to the opposite side of couple number three. Each couple in turn duck under the arch, pass through the lines, and arch at the head. The figure is repeated until all couples have passed through and formed an arch. Couple number one (the head couple) are now at the bottom of the line (Figure C).

Tunneling

Tunneling consists of couples passing under and through a tunnel—sometimes called the arch.

Tunneling is an excellent figure for breaking down the arch formation. The figure may begin at the head or at the foot of the line. We are going to describe the figure, beginning at the foot.

Partners stand in opposite lines, hands clasped in an arch formation, couple number one at the foot of the line.

Couple number one release hands, join inside hands, and ducking under couple number two, continue forward through the tunnel. As couple number one pass under the arch of couple number two, couple number two release hands, join inside hands, duck under the arch of couple number three, continuing forward behind couple number one (Figure D).

Each couple in turn break the arch, join inside hands, duck under, pass through the arch of the couple ahead, continuing forward.

Eventually couple number one become the head couple by passing through the entire line, and continue forward, the other couples following (Figure E).

The Star

This formation consists of lines converging toward a center, the inside persons joining hands, thus forming the star. When the inside persons clasp wrists with those opposite (in the center), the formation is known as the wagon wheel.

The trick of managing a good star formation consists of the inside persons marking time, while turning, the outer persons graduating the length of their stride.

A leader, however, should not attempt to call a star formation until the dancers have become experienced with the platoon formations.

20. Party Games

PARTY games are one of the most delightful customs carried over from the past. For generations couples have danced "Thread the Needle," "In and Out," "Wind the Spool," "Roll the Barrel," and "The Grapevine Twist." And today these party games are just as popular.

We are going to describe all of these figures. In addition to using these figures in social dancing, you will find them equally fitting for the square dances. In fact, the party figures are early American folk dances and are exhilarating for whatever occasion they are used.

THREAD THE NEEDLE

"Thread the Needle" consists of a leader, the group following, walking clockwise and through the end of a line, continuing forward in a circle so that each person is pulled into a right turn.

Starting with partners in an open circle facing in, arms raised, the hands joined, the woman standing on the right side of the man, the leader walks forward in a clockwise direction (Figure

A), the line following, and ducks under the arms of the end couple (Figure B). The leader continues forward in a clockwise direction, the line following pulling the man of the end couple into a right turn. Having snapped his right arm across his chest in turning, the end man now holds his partner's left hand in his right hand over his shoulder (Figure C). (The end woman remains in place in this position until she is joined by the leader toward the finish of the dance.)

The leader, the line following, repeats the figure continuing forward in a clockwise direction, ducking under the left arm of the end man and the right arm of the woman on his left (the woman in front). The line continues forward, pulling the woman into a right turn, and snapping her right arm across her chest, her right hand now clasping, at shoulder level, the left hand of the man behind.

The leader, the line following, continues to "thread the needle" (ducking under the arms of each couple) until each person has snapped about into a right turn, the right arm over the chest. To finish the figure the leader ducks under his own right arm, marches up to the end woman (the line following) and she places her right arm across her chest, clasping her right hand in the leader's left hand at shoulder level. The circle is now closed and the group may march forward or backward.

To resume a circle in which all are facing in, partners bring arms overhead while turning to the right, and lower arms. Everyone is now in original position.

IN AND OUT

The "In and Out" figure consists of a line weaving in and out between partners, each person turning inside out as the line passes through, and continuing forward in a counterclockwise direction.

Standing with partners in an open circle, arms slightly raised, hands joined, the woman on the right side of the man, the leader, moving in a counterclockwise direction (Figure A), ducks under the right arm of his partner, and continuing to move forward, pulls his partner inside out, the woman turning right under her right arm (Figure B). Continuing to draw his partner forward, the leader turns sharply to his left, ducks under the right arm of the next man (Figure C), pulling the man inside out, the man turning left under his right arm (Figure D). The line now continues, ducking under the right arm of the next woman, turning her inside out, the right arm of the next man, turning him inside out.

A

B

C

D

Ducking to the right and to the left continues until all partners have turned inside out. Eventually, everyone will be moving forward, the line facing out.

WIND THE SPOOL

(In "Winding the Spool" the leader should be careful not to bring the lines forming the concentric circles too close together by winding too tightly. In order to be able to unwind, he will have to allow sufficient leeway between the circles to allow him and the group following to pass between the lines.)

Starting with partners in an open circle, facing in, with hands joined, the woman on the right side of the man, the leader marches forward in a clockwise direction, the line following, and continues moving forward, making concentric circles until he reaches the center. The leader and the group have wound the spool and are now ready to unwind.

Unwind the Spool

To unwind the spool, the leader turns sharply to his left, the inside group following, and passes between the lines in a counter-clockwise direction until he resumes the single circle, all facing out.

By doing a sharp turn to the right, the group following, the leader may march forward until all are facing in.

ROLL THE BARREL

"Roll the Barrel" consists of turning a circle inside out and reversing the figure by turning outside in, so that partners are facing in the original formation.

Although any couple may roll the barrel, it will be simpler for someone to appoint a couple, naming an opposite couple who may roll the barrel in reverse. We will call the first couple A and the opposite couple B.

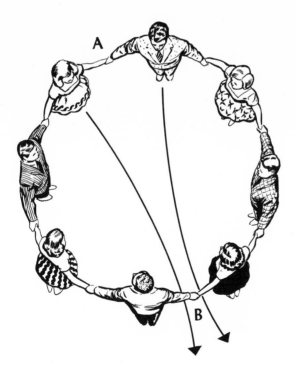

Standing with partners in a closed circle, hands joined, the woman on the right side of the man, couple A walk forward, drawing the group along in front of couple B who raise their arms to form an arch. Couple A pass through the arch, drawing the group forward, forcing couple B to turn inside out under their arms. Everyone is now facing out.

Roll the Barrel in Reverse

To roll the barrel in reverse couple B back up, drawing the group through the arch that has been formed by couple A. The group continues to back up, forcing couple A to turn outside in under their arms. Everyone is now facing in, in the original formation.

Now that you have learned to roll the barrel, try moving in a circle while doing the figure.

As the circle is turned inside out, keep moving in a circle to the right.

As the circle is turned outside in, keep moving in a circle to the left.

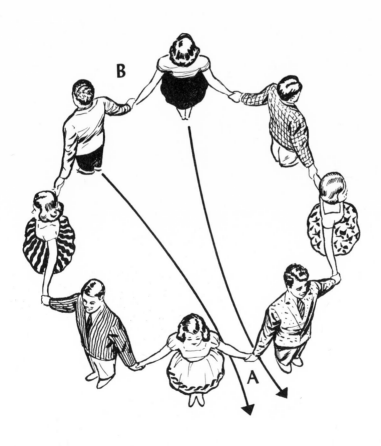

THE GRAPEVINE TWIST

"The Grapevine Twist" consists of a couple passing through a couple, circling around each partner, picking up the partners by joining hands, and moving on to the next couple. The leading couple continue (the others following) to weave in and out in the grapevine twist until all couples have been picked up.

Couples stand in a circle, slightly apart from each other, the woman on the right side of the man.

The leading couple, the man holding the woman's left hand in his right and drawing her after him, move to the couple on his right, pass between the couple, turn left around the woman, continuing left, pass between the couple, turn right around the man, and continue to the right (both couples joining hands), to visit the next couple.

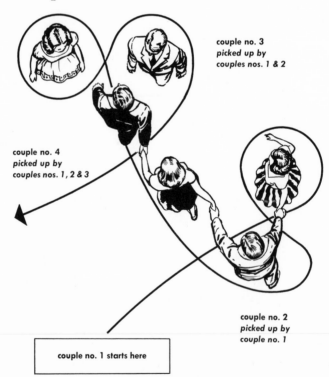

couple no. 3
picked up by
couples nos. 1 & 2

couple no. 4
picked up by
couples nos. 1, 2 & 3

couple no. 2
picked up by
couple no. 1

couple no. 1 starts here

The figure is repeated between and around each couple, the pickup occurring at the end of each grapevine twist. Eventually all couples will be drawn, with hands joined, into a circle.

SADIE HAWKINS

Although strictly speaking a Sadie Hawkins is not a party game, we are going to include it anyway because it's such fun.

A Sadie Hawkins consists of the women asking the men to be their partners at a dance. (After all, there is no reason why the men should always do the choosing.) Once in a while the women should have an opportunity to show their preferences, too. So try a Sadie Hawkins at your next dance.

21. Elimination Dances

THE elimination dance assumes an important role in any well-run dance. And everyone looks forward eagerly to the occasion.

The elimination dance differs from the mixers or party games in that couples are ruled out as the dance progresses. The process of elimination always creates an air of expectancy and suspense —the guests wondering who's next. Awarding a prize to the last couple on the floor adds further excitement. So you can see the elimination dance is a dramatic event on any program.

We are going to describe the following dances: the lucky-number, the flashlight, and the balloon dance. Before proceeding to the dances, we are going to discuss the role of the leader and the organization of props that may be used (numbers, prizes, etc.).

LEADER

Since there is always the element of the unpredictable even in an elimination dance, the leader will have to be ready for any emergency. The first problem he will have to face is the number of guests participating. With luck, he may start off with an equal number of couples, but as frequently happens, he may be faced with extra men or women. The only fair solution, in order to give everyone a chance to participate, is for the leader to give each extra man a number, in addition to the couples on the floor. As the first numbers are called, those couples surrender their number, and the extra man becomes the partner of the person just elimi-nated—both using the new number. This means, of course, that persons already eliminated will participate twice. But under the circumstances, it is unavoidable, and at least the extra man is given an opportunity to compete for a prize.

The running of an elimination dance requires expert timing on the part of the leader and a good, clear voice. A sense of humor helps, too! The leader can keep the dancers entertained while calling out the numbers. The most important thing, how-ever, is the speed with which the dance is run. Naturally, the guests who have already been eliminated, will lose interest if the dance is run too slowly. Even the fun of watching other couples being eliminated wears off if one remains a spectator for long. So the dance should be kept moving.

If properties are to be used, as for example, prizes and tickets in the lucky-number dance, the leader should have them well or-ganized in advance. There isn't a moment in which the leader can fumble about once the dancers have been called out on the floor. Therefore, two sets of numbers should be made in advance; one set to be distributed to the dancers—one number to a couple—and the second set to be retained by the leader, which he will use in reading off the numbers for the elimination dance.

If tickets (on which the numbers are written) are to be used, the leader would do well to appoint an assistant to collect the num-bers as the dancers are eliminated. An assistant can also see that the dancers do leave the floor after their number has been called.

If a band is accompanying the dancers, a leader will find it quite simple to stop the music as a number is called, or turn down the volume, by a mere signal of the hand. If records are used, however, the leader will be wise to appoint an assistant to handle the record machine.

Although it is optional with the leader whether or not a prize is given at the end of an elimination dance, a prize is an absolute must for the lucky-number dance. It is the star occasion, calling for that extra touch. Two prizes will have to be given—one to the woman and one to the man.

LUCKY-NUMBER DANCE

The lucky-number is the most popular of all the elimination dances. And it certainly provides the most suspense, combined with plenty of action.

The leader gives each couple a number. Everyone dances and as the music stops (or is turned down in volume), the leader calls out the first number to be eliminated. As the first couple drop out, the dance is resumed. The leader may now stop the dance and call several numbers in succession. (If a large group is participating, several numbers *should* be called in succession.) Couples continue to be eliminated until one couple remain on the floor. The last number is announced, the remaining couple becoming the winners. The lucky-number couple dance briefly for the spectators, and after the applause, are awarded the prize.

FLASHLIGHT DANCE

One or more flashlights may be used to eliminate the dancers from the floor. The room will have to be reasonably dark before the flashlight dance gets under way. Any couple spotted drop out automatically. The dance continues until all are eliminated.

The flashlight dance is one of the simplest to run. A leader, however, will have to use some caution in checking encumbrances around the room before the dance gets under way, since the dancers will be in semidarkness.

BALLOON DANCE

The balloon dance may be run in one of two ways. The balloons may be retained by the dancers as they are eliminated or the balloons may be broken as the numbers are called out. We are going to discuss the second method.

Each couple are given a number and a balloon. (The balloon may be attached to the ankle or carried in the hand.) While the dance is in progress the leader calls out a number. Everyone stops dancing to see whose number has been called. The unlucky couple begin to dodge about as the other couples move in. As soon as the balloon is broken, that couple are eliminated. The leader continues to call one number at a time, each couple in turn being eliminated as their balloon is broken.

The last couple have the privilege of retaining their balloon and may be given a prize.

In preparing for the balloon dance, the leader should make sure that the balloons are blown up and tied to strings in advance so that there will be no delay once the dance gets under way. A few spares (extra balloons) should be kept on hand in the event of an emergency. Even with the utmost caution, balloons have a way of blowing up!

22. Mixers

IF a committee or social director desires to keep a dance moving, it will be necessary to introduce an occasional mixer. (And as the word indicates, a mixer is a device for exchanging or meeting new partners.)

Certain couples tend to pair off for an entire dance, and however much fun they may have, other couples become bored with the same partners, and the dance begins to slump. It is at this point that a good social committee or leader steps in to call a mixer.

Aside from serving as a means of breaking up and exchanging partners, a mixer has an equally useful role to play in pulling a dance together at the slack periods. At the beginning of a dance, between dances, and after refreshments couples tend to wander off, so a mixer is an excellent device for gathering the group together.

Mixers, however, should be used sparingly. Too many mixers are as bad as too few. Guests, after all, have certain preferences as to partners, and if they are moved about indiscriminately and at too frequent intervals, the dance tends to disintegrate as the guests lose interest.

There are two types of mixers—those done without properties and those done with properties. We are going to describe the ones most commonly used. And since the mixers without props are the simplest to organize, we are going to describe them first. Here are the figures in order: circles, the basket (a variation of the double circle), concentric circles, the charge, backup, personality tie-ups, and the multiplication dance.

The mixers with props will follow. They will be discussed and described in the following order: pictures, cutting, the name mixer including a variation known as opposites, playing cards, string, and the broom dance.

MIXERS WITHOUT PROPERTIES

Circles

The simplest and quickest type of mixer is the circle. Guests may form single, double, or even concentric circles, if the group is large.

THE SINGLE CIRCLE

Partners form a circle, facing in, joining hands, the lady standing on the right side of her partner. At a signal the leader may say, "Gentlemen dance with the lady on your left." After the new partners have danced together, the leader may call, "Everyone back in the circle—your new partner on your right." After the group assembles in the circle, the leader may add, "Everyone grab your opposite." The dancers rush across the floor and grab a new partner. After a brief dance the leader may call, "Everyone back in the circle with your original partner at your side—now dance with your own partner."

Any number of variations in the calls may be made by the leader to mix up the guests.

THE DOUBLE CIRCLE

Ladies form a circle, facing in, and join hands. The men form an outer circle, facing in, standing behind the ladies with hands joined.

At a signal from the leader the men move sideward in a counterclockwise direction, the ladies moving sideward in a clockwise direction. As the circles move in opposition the leader calls out, "Stop." Ladies turn around and face a partner, both circles coming to a halt. The leader follows with the call, "Everybody dance."

As soon as the dancers have become familiar with the preceding routine, there is an even more interesting way in which they may do the double circle mixer. It is a progressive mixer and is by far the most popular. The leader explains in advance that the ladies will meet three different men as they move in opposite directions, each of whom will become their partner in succession. No one dances with a partner until the signal "Stop" has been called three times, at the end of which signal the dancers scramble to find partners. After dancing briefly with partners number one, the dancers proceed, at a signal from the leader, to find partners number two and dance again. Releasing partners number two, the dancers, at the signal, progress to partners number three and finish the dance.

This progressive mixer is so well liked that longer periods of dancing may be done with a given partner instead of the usual brief episodes. Three dances, for example, may be done in succession without anyone losing interest. In that way the program will not become too set or routine. And everyone will be happy.

BASKET

For variety the basket formation may be used while the dancers are in a double circle.

At the signal "Form a basket" the men raise their arms as the ladies duck under to stand between and slightly behind the men. The leader now calls to the men, "The first partner will be the lady on your right, the second partner the lady on your left. Now everybody dance!" The men dance with partners number one and leave them to dance with partners number two at a signal from the leader.

CONCENTRIC CIRCLES

Concentric circles may be formed when the group is large. Several circles can be formed, facing in, the men standing behind the ladies. It is wise for the leader to keep the figures and signals simple. A large group becomes unwieldy when the mixer becomes too involved. Depending on the size of the room, any number of dancers may participate.

Personality Tie-Ups

Guests will have a great deal of fun doing this mixer in which one exchanges partners on the basis of the color of eyes or hair or even clothes. The leader may call out, for example, "Everyone with blue eyes dance with partners who have brown eyes." Or the call may be, "Brunettes dance with blondes." (Anyone who doesn't fall into this category, for example, a redhead, may grab anyone who has got lost in the shuffle.)

The periods of dancing should be kept brief so that the calls can be changed constantly. Everyone will enjoy being in a happy state of confusion while looking for the next partner. And the calls should be so varied that the dancers will be keyed up for the next stunt. By all means keep the dancers in a state of expectancy—otherwise the personality mixer will fall flat.

Multiplication Dance

The multiplication dance, as the name might suggest, consists of partners dancing and adding other couples to the floor, progressively.

It is by far the most dramatic of all the mixers. And it has real audience appeal. Each person enjoys having spectators look on as he or she is chosen, and it's always fun to show off one's dancing ability after one is chosen.

In running the multiplication dance, the leader should make the periods quite brief so that couples who are seated may join the dance quickly. If the dance is not run at a good, snappy pace the spectators lose interest.

The multiplication dance begins with one couple dancing. At a signal from the leader the music stops, partners break away and each finds a new partner. (Only people who are seated may be asked.) Two couples now dance on the floor until the music stops when the signal is given for the next set of partners. Four couples now join the dance. Each time that the music stops, partners break away and find new partners. As you can see, each time the dance is resumed the number of couples is doubled. The dance is continued until everyone is on the floor.

MIXERS WITH PROPERTIES

Props such as pictures, playing cards, names, etc., always dress up a dance and provide dramatic interest. They may be used as a device to pull a dance together, as a means of rotating and meeting new partners, and may even be used for cutting in.

A leader can have a wonderful time varying the mixers we are about to describe. And for a leader with imagination, the possibilities for new and creative ideas are endless.

However gay and festive props may make a mixer, there is a practical side to be considered. The leader will have to organize or execute all props to be used before the dance. A wise leader, therefore, will appoint a committee from among the group.

None of the property mixers we are about to describe entail any real expense. But make no mistake—plenty of time is required to make up the ingredients for some of the mixers. Materials will have to be collected well in advance of the dance and sufficient leeway allowed for actually making the props.

The mixers that require time are the picture mixer, string mixer, and especially the name mixer. The leader or committee should have all the implements necessary for carrying out the scheme—scissors, paper, crayons, balloons, etc. And everything should be so neatly tucked away that a leader can pull out props for use at a moment's notice.

The property mixers that are simple and easy to plan are playing cards, lemons, apples, flowers, lollipops, etc., and, of course, the perennial broom!

In running a property mixer the leader should make a careful count of the number of partners on the floor. The number of props to be distributed can then be allocated in advance.

And now we are ready for these delightful mixers.

Pictures

The most popular property mixer is the picture mixer. The leader distributes pictures that have been cut in half—one half of the pictures going to the ladies, the other half of the same pictures going to the men. The object of the dance is to match up the pictures to find partners. As soon as all the pictures have been matched up, the dance gets under way.

In making up the picture mixer the leader should use big, bold colored pictures. (Stay away from black and white prints.) The pictures, before being cut up, should be marked across the back with a heavy crayon—an X will do—so that the dancers will not be confused as to which side is the picture. A generous number of pictures should be kept on hand so that the pictures can be rotated when in constant use.

Cutting (with Properties)

If one has to give up a partner, it's easier to do so gracefully if one is presented with a prop as amusing as a lemon, an apple, a lollipop, or a surprise ball (crepe paper).

All of the preceding props are handed to the extra ladies or men as a dance gets under way. At the close of any dance, the props are returned to the leader.

The Name Mixer

The name mixer is especially appealing because of the personal touch—of finding the name of a friend or, perhaps, someone else finding one's own name in an envelope, a balloon, a lollipop, or even an apple—the object of the mixer being, as usual, the finding of a partner. (For the more formal dances, name cards may be inserted in envelopes or even tucked into paper flowers.) For example, the men can be presented by the leader with the ladies' names on slips of paper, which may or may not be tucked into a prop. As soon as the lady's name is discovered, the man claims her as his partner. After all the names have been discovered, partners pair off for the dance.

Opposites

The name mixer need not be confined to personal names. For variety, the names of celebrities, or slogans or popular songs could be substituted. Opposites, then, is a variation of the name mixer.

When opposites is used as a mixer, two slips of paper are made for each couple—one slip for the lady and one slip for the man. Half of a name or slogan is printed on one slip, the remaining half on a second slip, for example, pepper and salt. If a man receives "pepper," he looks for his opposite, the lady who has received "salt." She becomes his partner. Opposites continue to look for each other until all the couples are matched off. The dance then gets under way.

Here is a partial list of opposites that have been found the most amusing:

HOT	— DOG
BEAUTY AND THE	— BEAST
HOT AND	— COLD
COCA	— COLA
SEVEN	— UP
NIGHT AND	— DAY
HAMBURGER WITH	— ONIONS
APPLE PIE WITH	— CHEESE
HOT FUDGE	— SUNDAE
ETC., ETC.	

Playing Cards

Playing cards are always amusing when used as a mixer. The leader deals out the pack to the dancers, hearts and diamonds to the ladies, clubs and spades to the men. The object of the dance is to match up cards to find partners—hearts and clubs matching and similarly, diamonds and spades. For example, if a lady has a queen of hearts card, she pairs off with the man who has a queen of clubs. Cards with corresponding numbers are also matched. The hunt continues until everyone has found a partner.

The String

The string mixer consists of the ladies tying strings on their little fingers, about two yards in length, putting their hands behind their backs, the opposite end of the strings being looped together and held by the leader in one hand. At a signal the men rush up, and choosing a string, pull slightly to determine who is the owner. As soon as the man has discovered the owner, he dances with that lady. Each man in turn keeps pulling a string until every lady has been discovered.

The string mixer is especially suitable for a small group. If a leader is faced with a larger group, it will be wise to seek the assistance of several people who can help distribute the strings among smaller units. Since it does take time to distribute and to tie the strings, much time will be saved if this procedure is adopted.

Broom Dance

The broom dance continues to be the favorite with everyone. And it does add spice to any dance. The broom dance has a practical aspect, however, which is the sure-fire solution for that extra man.

A leader gives the broom to the person without a partner as couples assemble on the floor. (The broom is carried in front with both hands clasping the handle.) The music begins, and as the dance progresses, the leader signals to the dancer with the broom to drop it. (A *reasonable* bang will do!) As the broom falls to the floor, everybody rushes to grab a new partner. The person left without a partner picks up the broom and dances with it as the other couples continue to dance.

Once the dance has got under way, the person dancing with the broom may drop it at any moment. However, the broom should not be dropped too frequently or the dance falls apart. What is equally important, the broom should not be kept by one person for to long a period. Although the object of the broom dance is to get a partner, apparently the broom is more popular. So give everyone a chance!

23. Invitations

INVITATIONS to a dance are usually offered through the medium of the telephone or written word.

At all times, you, the recipient, are under obligation to accept or reject within a reasonable time. The type of invitation will indicate how to dress. (When in doubt, always inquire of your host or hostess.)

Informal written invitations may be handled through a name card or letter, and should include information indicating time, place, etc. The recipient can respond through telephone, own name card, or letter.

The formal invitation is written, printed, or engraved, and written acknowledgment is customary.

Miss Betty White
requests the pleasure of —————'s
company at a dance to be held at

————————————————

at —————*o'clock in the evening,*
(day of month) —————————.

(Spell out time and date.)

Reply:

Mr.——accepts with pleasure
Miss Betty White's invitation
to a dance to be held at

_____

at ——o'clock in the evening,
(day of month) ——————.

(Spell out time and date.)

24. At the Dance

UPON ARRIVING

Having disposed of wraps as soon as you are admitted, you will want to find your hostess and greet her.

ON THE FLOOR

If the dance is not already in progress, you may wish to wander around with your escort and visit with your friends.

When you are ready to begin your first dance (and it should be with your escort), the procedure is for the man to ask, "May I have this dance?" or, "Will you dance with me?" (Either form is acceptable.)

After you have finished a dance you should thank your partner, and she in turn should reciprocate with some sort of pleasantry. If you are not going to stay with your partner, you should return her to her own group or leave her comfortably seated with her friends. (At no time should a woman be left standing alone on the floor.) Remember, it is as important to observe good social custom at a dance as to be able to dance well. However, there are occasional lapses on the part of some guests, such as: slighting one person in order to dance with another, becoming a dance exhibitionist, or criticizing one's partner. The partner who is popular and sought after, however, recognizes the importance of avoiding these situations.

As has already been indicated, the man assumes entire responsibility for his partner. Therefore, he should keep an eye out for what is going on in general. It will help considerably when the social director or hostess is ready to call a mixer or any other gathering of the group.

If cutting in is permitted, the usual customs should be observed: circulating on the outside of the dance floor, lightly touching the shoulder of the man you are cutting in on, with the customary "May I?" and not cutting back on the same man.

If you wish to share refreshments with your partner you should reserve with her the dance just before an intermission.

UPON LEAVING

It is customary to have the last dance with one's escort. Upon leaving, you should single out your hostess to express your appreciation for the success of the dance. If the hostess is engaged it is perfectly acceptable to express your pleasure to a member of the social committee.